DATE DUE

OVERDUE FINE
$0.10 PER DAY

DEMCO

Advance praise for
Watch Me Grow: I'm Two

"This second book in the Watch Me Grow series is an exceptional resource for all parents. Dr. O'Brien's words encourage parents to embrace the unique and individual behaviors of their child. You feel comforted and nurtured by her understanding of the challenges and frustrations in parenting a two-year-old. I will recommend this book to my child life students who are preparing to work with children and families."

—CLAIRE M. WHITE, M.S., C.C.L.S., assistant professor of child life, Wheelock College

"As the father of five children long past age two, I remember enough about those years to know how much this book would have helped us and any parent. This book is wisdom well told."

—DAVID LAWRENCE, JR., president, The Early Childhood Initiative Foundation

"Dr. O'Brien and Ms. Tippins have written a warm and comprehensive view of the wonder of development in the two-year-old. They bring this development continuum to life by providing a 'peek' into the child's development and behavior in the context of family interactions and activities. Every parent can relate to these scenarios that bring a sometimes humorous but always enlightening view of life with a terrific two-year-old."

—DR. KRISTIE BRANDT, Napa County Health & Human Services

"As a parent and a professional I found the book to be enlightening and compelling. O'Brien's conversational style is effective in communicating complex developmental theory in a manner easily understood by parents and preschool educators. O'Brien strikes the perfect balance between theory and practice as it pertains to the parenting role in facilitating child development, and parents will recognize the many developmental milestones addressed through the use of touching anecdotes. This is a must-read for the parents of a two-year-old."

—GREGORY HALL, chair, Department of Behavioral Sciences, Bentley College

WATCH ME GROW:

I'm Two

Every Parent's Guide to the
Lively & Challenging
24- to 36-Month-Old

MAUREEN O'BRIEN, Ph.D.,
WITH **SHERILL TIPPINS**

WM
WILLIAM MORROW
75 YEARS OF PUBLISHING
An Imprint of HarperCollins*Publishers*

A SKYLIGHT PRESS BOOK

HarperCollins books may be purchased for educational, business, or sales promotional use. For information please write: Special Markets Department, HarperCollins Publishers Inc., 10 East 53rd Street, New York, NY 10022.

FIRST EDITION

Photographs by Elise Sinagra Donoghue

Designed by Gretchen Achilles

Printed on acid-free paper

Library of Congress Cataloging-in-Publication Data has been applied for.

ISBN 0-688-16879-5

01 02 03 04 05   QW   10 9 8 7 6 5 4 3 2 1

TO MOM

and all the other moms out there who are the heart

of their children's future

CONTENTS

ACKNOWLEDGMENTS

All of the books in the Watch Me Grow series owe their essence to my personal and professional experiences with mentors, as well as the deep wisdom of other parents. My years spent with colleagues at the Touchpoints Project (now the Brazelton Touchpoints Center) at Children's Hospital in Boston are the most recent example. My graduate training at Temple University and the Institute of Child Development at the University of Minnesota continues to inform my understanding of parenting issues.

The Watch Me Grow books are a collaborative effort, with several "partners." Foremost, Sherill Tippins is a wondrous writing partner—insightful, humorous, and real. Elise Donoghue's photographs bring the stories to life. Lynn Sonberg and Meg Schneider of Skylight Press and Betty Kelly and her team at HarperCollins/William Morrow round out the "behind the scenes" supporters. Thanks also to the folks who graciously opened their doors for photos: the Boston Children's Museum, Bright Horizons, Children First, Lori Mitcheroney, and numerous parents.

Last, thanks to my husband, George, for his steady encouragement, and to my kids, Alex and Matthew. They continually delight me with the joy of discovery that parenting brings.

—MAUREEN O'BRIEN

Watch Me Grow:
I'm Two

Introduction

"I don't know if I can take it anymore," the woman in line at the grocery store murmured to her friend. "It took me an hour to get out of the house this morning because Darcy absolutely refused to get dressed. I'd been late for work on Monday for the same reason. I could just imagine the look on my boss's face if he saw me walk in late again. I was so desperate I offered to put Darcy in her best velvet party dress if she'd just let me cover her body with something— but all she did was hide under the covers, wailing, 'No! No! No!'"

The woman's friend lifted her eyebrows in a world-weary way. "She wanted to wear the shirt and pants she wore yesterday, right? The cruddy ones in the laundry hamper?"

The first woman laughed in surprise. "How did you know?"

Her friend shrugged. "Darcy's two."

Hearing this conversation, I couldn't help but sympathize with the mother (what parent doesn't know how frustrated she felt that morning?), but I could see poor Darcy's side, too. It can't always be fun to be labeled part of the "terrible twos" club, whose members are best known for their stubbornness, defiance, and (worst of all) public temper tantrums. No doubt, there were times when Darcy brought great joy to her mother—by shrieking with delight at the sight of a bright balloon, proudly showing off her latest crayon creation, or solemnly telling her parents how much she loves them—but in the rush and pressure of everyday life it is sometimes hard to recall those wonderful moments our children share with us. Two-year-olds can especially try our patience as their improving verbal, physical, and emotional skills make them seem more capable of responding appropriately than they really are. Darcy may have listened attentively as her mother explained that she had to get dressed *now* because Mommy had to get to work on time, but at two she was far from understanding the concept of "getting to work," much less the idea of "on time." Instead, she may have latched on to the memory of how uncomfortably clothes could rub against her skin, decided that she wanted to run and jump freely that morning without being encased in a dress, or resisted cooperating in a certain sequence of events she knew would lead to her mother's departure. Her need to establish her own identity by getting her way may have prevented her from going along with her mother even though she wanted her approval. Unfortunately, at Darcy's age, the only way she could express these intense feelings was to scrunch up her face in defiance and shout, "No!" In other words, the business of being two may be keeping her from getting what she wants nearly as often as it frustrates her mom.

As Darcy's mother and her friend left the store, I thought about all the advice the mother would probably get from well-meaning friends, television, and parenting books and magazines on how to get her toddler to behave. Some of the advice would be good, some bad, but chances are that little if any would be tailored to the needs or circumstances of her particular child. If only someone could help that mother see what caused *her* child's behavior at a given time, I thought—if only she could step back and observe the ways in which her daughter's developmental level, emotional needs, and unique personality meld or collide with those of her caregivers—that mother would be well on her way to creating parenting strategies that actually work.

My goal with this book, as with all the books in the *Watch Me Grow* series, is to help you step back as a parent and take a look at *your* child's mind, emotions, and abilities at each phase of development. Only in this way can you begin to understand why your child's behavior appears so remarkably mature at times (comforting a younger child who is crying) but can be so maddening a few hours later (throwing a cup across the room). As a developmental psychologist and researcher, former director of Boston's Brazelton Touchpoints Center, and a university professor, I am well aware of the vast and growing body of research on how young children learn and grow. As the mother of twin seven-year-old boys, I know from personal experience that children are very different from one another, even when they are the same age or in the same family; that they are *growing, changing* beings whose comprehension, skills, needs, and desires evolve over time; and that parenting itself is a constant challenge that can be eased (but not erased) as parents grow to understand more about their particular child.

Not so many years ago, children were seen—by scientists, child development experts, and many parents—as empty vessels waiting to be filled. Recent research into the workings of the developing brain has challenged this assumption, showing that young children are more actively engaged with the world, deliberately interacting with their environment in ways that literally shape their brains. Now that your two-year-old can move about on his own, he is even less dependent on your constant, methodical "teaching" than he was a year ago. Problem-solving and mastery of skills will be his major agenda for the year. Of course, you will want to be there to reinforce what he is learning, but he will lead the way much more often than he used to as he explores the world around him. Parenting a two-year-old is all about this interplay between following and leading—knowing when to let your child make discoveries on his own, and when to elaborate on those discoveries to bring him forward a little bit more.

The key to raising any child successfully lies in observing him accurately, with an educated eye, and then using your knowledge of his temperament, history, and capabilities to help him create what the psychologist Jerome Bruner calls a secure scaffolding that will support his climb toward adulthood. In these pages, I walk with you through the practical situations that you encounter with your child every day. It is my hope that this book will enhance the life of your two-year-old and your entire family, helping you grow together with greater understanding, excitement, and joy.

CHAPTER 1

What I'm Like

Your child is able to take the initiative in learning much more than before. The art of parenting lies in supporting her interests as they develop.

It's hard to believe how much a twenty-four-month-old has already learned about how the world works, what kinds of pleasure, support, and stimulation it can offer her and the many exciting ways she can interact with it. As Maggie and Richard Wolff sit down to dinner with six-year-old Justin and two-year-old Amy in her booster seat, they exchange a glance of relief mixed with pride. Finally, after all the months of milky spit-ups, interrupted sleep, teething dramas, and wordless wails, the Wolffs are starting to look like a functional family again—four individuals with distinct personalities and increasingly effective ways of communicating their needs. Even mealtime seems on the verge of becoming an enriching family activity, rather than a rushed attempt to bolt down food while Amy tries to tip her high chair over or throws her food. As Amy announces, "Butter, pease," stretching out her hand as elegantly as a princess, Maggie dares to look ahead to dinner-times filled with conversations about each family member's day, perhaps even ending with an offer from the kids to help clean up. She gives her daughter a smile. *Look at her,* Maggie thinks. *She's practically a little girl already. Her hair's all the way down to her shoulders. She sits up straighter in her chair. Her gaze is just as direct and confident as Justin's!*

"Let me help you butter that roll," Richard says to Amy, holding the butter dish in one hand and reaching for Amy's plate with the other.

Instantly, Amy grabs the edge of her plate. "No!" she yells. "*My* dish!"

Uh-oh. Maggie's heart sinks. That tone of voice is certainly familiar, and Maggie notes that Amy's hunger is what's really getting in the way of her patience. "Amy, let your father butter the roll for you," she says, hoping for the best. "He'll put plenty on, just like you want it."

"*I* do it! Gimme!" Amy's face, scrunched up like a samurai warrior's, has turned bright red. She opens her mouth, and the entire family flinches in the face of her bloodcurdling scream. Her brother rolls his eyes. "Can I be excused?" he asks.

"Amy, let . . . me . . . have . . . the . . . plate." Richard tugs on the dish with each word. But his daughter pulls back. A moment later, the inevitable happens: the dish goes flying off the table, and the family dog pounces on the unexpected treat.

As Maggie and Richard resignedly clean up the mess, order Justin back to his seat, and try to salvage the rest of dinnertime, Maggie has to admit to her husband and herself that, "after all, Amy *is* only two."

However bright their daughter is, and however amazing her progress has been from dependent infant to active, independent toddler, she still has much learning and development ahead of her in all realms—emotion, self-expression, social interaction, advanced thinking, and motor skills. The adults around her, naturally impressed by her advances so far, may assume that she comprehends and is capable of doing more than she really can. But as every parent learns, a two-year-old can *say,* "I do it," but that doesn't mean she can *accomplish* a particular action. She says, "Okay," when you tell her to put her shoes on, but she doesn't necessarily understand that you mean right *now.* She knows what she wants, but she is still often unable to express her desire acceptably in words.

In fact, the central dilemma for both child and parent in the third year springs largely from the normal unevenness of a two-year-old's mental, physical, and emotional development. Although a child this age is certainly making marvelous progress, she still has quite a short attention span, a limited ability to postpone gratification and to plan for the future, and a need for time and patience when learning to dress herself, follow daily routines, share with others, and express her feelings. She still must rely on her caregivers' emotional, educational, and practical support to ease her into early childhood *as she becomes ready,* and not before. Many of the difficulties that so commonly occur during this year—conflicts that can lead to furious impatience on the parents' part and loss of control (and even tantrums) on the child's part—are a result of this mismatch between a parent's or child's expectations and the child's abilities.

Fortunately, the third year of life is a time of profound growth in just those areas that can seem so defeating right around her second birthday. Last year you were able to encourage and applaud your child's very clear triumphs in learning to walk and to say her first words. This year her deepening awareness and refinement of skills may not be as easy to observe, but these advances will improve all of your lives in very important ways. At age one, her one- or two-word utterances frequently left you fishing for their meaning; this year she will learn to express, in increasingly varied sentences, more of what she thinks and feels. At age one, she could sit at the dinner table (in a high chair or booster seat) but did not fully participate in the ritual of the meal. By the end of this year, she will be able to listen to her brother's tales about his school day and perhaps chime in with a simple story of her own ("I went to the zoo. There was giraffes!"). The first, rather awkward play dates of her second year may progress toward budding friendships in her third. And of course, last year's early attempts to establish who she is will lead to this year's full-blown tests of the limits of acceptable behavior and the power of her individual will. Your two-year-old's progress, in other words, will be more a matter of depth than breadth. As the months pass, you'll experience the pleasure of watching her consolidate, integrate, and act on all the knowledge she has acquired, until she is able to master her world and herself with the true dexterity of a growing child.

A CHILD'S-EYE VIEW
"Mommy Home!"

Twenty-four-month-old Isabel is playing with blocks on the living room floor. *Yellow block on top,* she tells herself. She feels happy and busy, sharing her toys with her mom, Diane, who sits stretched out beside her. As she balances a third wooden cube on top of the yellow one, she proudly announces, "Tree bocks!" and enjoys a surge of satisfaction as Mommy applauds.

Just then, she hears the sound of a key in the front door lock. Her hand freezes, hovering over the pile of blocks. *What's that noise?* She searches her memory. *Key in the lock means Mommy's home from work.* She looks at her mother. "Mommy home!" she says with a big smile.

Mommy looks very surprised. "No, silly," she says. "Mommy's right here. That's Daddy!"

Isabel blinks, acknowledging this contradiction between a learned association (key in the lock equals Mommy) and the evidence her mom presents ("Mommy's right here"). The door opens, and she turns toward it to see her father entering the room. Isabel's eyes widen. She looks back at Mommy. "Yay!" she says brightly, demonstrating her deeper understanding of this particular situation. "Daddy home!"

"LOOK AT ME!": YOUR CHILD'S PROGRESS IN THE THIRD YEAR

What great satisfaction we parents take in watching our two-year-olds run, jump, and climb on the little kids' playground, almost as independently as the big kids nearby. The pride they take in their own accomplishments, so obvious each time they rush back to give us a progress report, is hard-won and certainly deserved. Consider the fact that only eighteen months ago your child was just beginning to sit up, babble nonsense sounds, and grasp objects within her reach. She's been walking for only a year or less, and speaking in sentences just recently if at all. As she neared her second birthday, she grew somewhat more aware of the world outside her immediate environment—its attractions, its mysteries, and the other people inhabiting it. Now, early in her third year, she can walk, run, and climb with ease, speak more clearly and be understood, and perceive that others' viewpoints may differ from her own. She stands poised on the brink of true individuality—ready to take her place as a unique member of her world.

Your child will accomplish this feat by continuing to refine a wide variety of skills over the next twelve months, as well as develop some new abilities. As we will see in Chapter 2, her change in physical appearance from potbellied toddler to straight-backed young child during the first half of this year will accompany a similar progression in such gross-motor skills as walking, running, climbing, pushing, and pulling. Delighting in her new sense of physical power, she will soon start to experiment with new variations in movement—trying a somersault after seeing one on TV, spinning in place and falling down dizzy, and squatting and waddling like a duck. Her fine-motor skills—buttoning, cutting, drawing, threading—will progress even more dramatically this year, leading inevitably to demands to "do it myself." One of the most welcome aspects of this new self-sufficiency involves her physiological development. By the middle of the year, if not before, your child will be able to control her bladder sufficiently to allow toilet training to begin, and her drive toward independence may motivate her to go to the bathroom "like the big kids." At the best of times, her burgeoning abilities in all of these areas will lessen her frustration level (and your own). Still, you will want to build in the extra minutes she'll need to try to dress herself, eat meals without help, and help her little brother drink from his bottle.

Just as daily practice improves your two-year-old's motor skills, continued experimentation with objects and people enhances her understanding of her world in new, exciting ways. In Chapter 3, we will trace the two-year-old's journey from simple planning and problem-solving toward a more complex and sophisticated ability to imagine, pretend, and express herself in words and in play. Her world, once an unknown expanse, is now filled with familiar, reassuring landmarks. Her sense of time may have also developed to the point where she understands the concepts of "later," "soon," and "in just a minute," though she still can't wait very long to get what she wants. Her attention span will lengthen considerably this year, as will her ability to notice more than one aspect of an object or situation at a time—two skills that help her follow storylines, make multistep plans, and retain memories for longer periods. Like a child coloring in the outlines in a coloring book, your two-year-old will continue to fill in the details of her immediate environment as the year progresses. She will grow increasingly eager to explore the larger world beyond her front door. Her expanding curiosity may even enable her to benefit from a preschool program or other regular group activity this year.

Your child's cognitive development may reveal itself most clearly in her amazing verbal growth. Not only will her vocabulary grow at a truly astronomical rate, but, as we will see in Chapter 5, she will begin to demonstrate her comprehension of many of the basic rules of grammar as she speaks in sentences of three, four, and even more words. "No nap" will become "I don't want nap," "All wet" will grow to "Look, it's all wet!" and "Baba juice" will develop into "More juice, peeze." From this point onward, her verbal repertoire will expand exponentially, not only in the quantity of her words but in the quality and range of her expression. By the end of the year, you are likely to have a real conversationalist on your hands.

Despite these advances in your child's verbal abilities, she will not always be able to express the frustration she feels at not being able to master her entire world. For this reason, you are likely to hear "No!" and witness angry outbursts even more often after she turns two. In Chapter 5, we will see how, as my colleagues at Touchpoints have shown, temporary surges in cognitive development (speech, concepts) or physical changes (toilet training) may disrupt sleep or lead to emotional scenes. Fortunately, as your child's ability to express herself improves, and as she grows better able to wait for what she wants and accept the fact that others may have a different point of view, her negative behavior will gradually abate. By age three, her emotional life will have grown more complex, encompassing new feelings such as shame, embarrassment, and true pride. She will be better able to show empathy for others and will probably begin to demonstrate a budding sense of humor. Her personality will have established itself, enabling you to better understand her and thus weather the inevitable storms. In fact, her heightened desire to live up to your standards may well lead to a "second honeymoon" of closeness between you and your child.

Your two-year-old's efforts to know and express herself more fully will be enhanced by new relationships with others. During this year, she will begin to pay more attention to the children around her, learning a great deal from them through imitation. In Chapter 6, we will explore ways parents can build on these experiences when reinforcing social rules, including taking turns, sharing, and refraining from aggression. We will see how games and other play activities can also teach these conventions, and we will discuss ways in which your child's new, often highly simplified ideas about boys and girls can be gently guided and shaped. We will also look at the issues of morality and empathy for others and discuss ways to lay the groundwork for this development.

As your two-year-old grows in all of these ways—as she learns to communicate more effectively, wait a bit longer for a treat, and enjoy interacting with her peers—you can bolster her confidence through a support system of daily routines, clear rules, and simple methods for resolving conflicts. Chapters 7 and 8 explore ways to create predictable, but not rigid, structures for such two-year-old challenges as bedtime, dinnertime, and toilet training, as well as ways to cope with behavior that has gotten out of hand.

Of course, life with a two-year-old rarely proceeds according to

plan. Discipline issues, disruptions to routine, and uneven development all occur frequently enough to challenge even the most saintly
parent's patience. It helps to remind yourself ahead of time that exceptions will surface for every rule—that behavior will sometimes turn
erratic, plans will have to be scrapped, and your child will not always
"perform" as you would like. Children differ in the areas of development they choose to work on at any particular time. Your friend's
twenty-four-month-old may be willing to experiment with taking
turns and sharing or otherwise develop her social skills, while yours
refuses to do so but is moving along faster in her climbing, hopping,
and balancing abilities. Never fear—the two children will switch
places more than once in the year to come. During this period when
your child moves productively from one type of growth to another and
then back again, it's important not to "type" her too soon (announcing,
for example, that "Rose is a great athlete but not very social"). As a
two-year-old, she is able to lead the way in her own learning much
more than before. The art of parenting lies in observing her interests as
they occur, and arranging her world so that she can make many of her
discoveries on her own.

A PARENT'S STORY
Thinking Like a Toddler

"I'd always heard that girls were better at toilet training than
boys," a woman reported at a parenting group meeting I vis-
ited recently. "I was really glad to hear it, because I wanted to
put my daughter Denise in a preschool program that doesn't
accept kids in diapers. About six months before Denise was due
to start the program, I began the whole process—giving her a
potty to sit on, reading her books about using the potty, asking
older kids to let her watch them use the potty, buying her flow-
ery little underpants to wear instead of diapers, and so on.
Denise is a smart girl. I figured if I just followed all the steps,
so to speak, everything would work out fine.

"But no matter how much I talked about how great that potty was, Denise just would not use it. The weeks passed, and I was at my wit's end. I'd already put down the deposit for the preschool, and I was scared to lose it. Then one day, about two weeks before preschool started, Denise and I were walking through Macy's children's department, and she suddenly stopped dead in her tracks. "Superman!" she said. I looked where she was pointing, and there was a pair of blue and red Superman underwear lying on a pile of clothes in a sale bin. And it hit me—the little boy next door who'd let her watch him use the bathroom was wearing Superman underwear at the time. He'd done a whole Superman act for Denise that day that had really entranced her. Naturally, I bought half a dozen pairs of that underwear right then and took them home—and from the time I put a pair on her, Denise started really trying to use the potty, just like the boy next door. Apparently, she'd made a strong connection in her mind between Superman underwear and using the bathroom, but I'd never have been able to take advantage of it if I hadn't finally listened to her and followed her lead."

"NOW I UNDERSTAND": HOW YOUR CHILD'S COMPREHENSION GROWS

One of the most gratifying aspects of your child's development this year is her increased ability to make associations—to connect one piece of information with another in her mind and use that link to create new ideas and concepts about her world. Some of these associations lead to truly impressive leaps of insight. A two-year-old might put a handful of snow in her mouth, for example, and when asked what she is eating, answer, "Water." Other links, such as a new ability to see the number 1 on a page and say the word, will pave the way to a higher order of learning. Some connections are so wildly fanciful that they charm us with their originality even as we wonder how they ever occurred—as when a

You can almost see "the wheels turn" inside your two-year-old's head as she valiantly tries to solve new dilemmas.

child urged to look at a video camera and say hi to Grandma asks, "Is Grandma in *there?*"

The ability to associate one observation or idea with another is enhanced by your toddler's longer memory and attention span. When she can *remember* the golden retriever your friend Susan brought to visit last week, it's easier for her to link it to the dog she sees in a neighbor's yard this afternoon ("Look! Susan dog!"). When she is able to spend more than a minute or so *focusing* on one object, she is likely to notice more aspects of that object that she can connect with something else ("Doggie has tail—like my kitty!"). Her ability to *classify* objects (this is a dog, not a horse) will also increase significantly this year, helping her to develop general assumptions about all the members of a group ("Dogs like bones") and to predict sequences ("I throw the ball. Daddy catch it"). A two-year-old's verbal development greatly enhances her ability to comprehend and retain the hundreds of associations she makes each day. As she moves through this year, you are likely to see her literally narrating her actions ("Punch the dough!" "Up the steps, up the steps, up the steps . . .") as she learns to link her physical movements with mental activity. All of these links not only stimulate her cognitive development but spur her imagination as she links your behavior toward her with her own behavior toward her dolly, or when she pretends to rake leaves just like Daddy did last weekend.

Amazingly, the countless associations you can see your two-year-old making represent only the tip of the iceberg as far as her mental activity is concerned. Because two-year-olds are still able to communicate only a small portion of what they're thinking, most of their associations take place invisibly. Only recently, as researchers have come up with better-designed experiments and studies, have we begun to realize that toddlers understand, analyze, and retain much more than they have traditionally been given credit for. In short, the two-year-old's "associative machine" virtually never stops working. As a result, this is a year when you as a parent can contribute a great deal to your child's learning. By keeping an eye (and ear) out for the associations that your child expresses, and making the right comments to extend them ("You're right, snow becomes water. The hot sun—or your warm tongue—melts it"), you can stimulate her thinking even more. Certainly, her brain is ripe for such nourishment. A two-year-old's brain is 75 percent as large as an adult's; by age three it will have grown to 90 percent of adult size.

EASING THE WAY
Playing Isn't Everything

Parents are not (usually) preschool teachers, and it isn't necessary or even wise to spend all of your time down on the floor deliberately stimulating your child through games, artwork, play, and other child-centered activities. Children make associations no matter what's going on around them. As long as you and your child spend your time together actively observing and commenting on your surroundings, she can learn an enormous amount by, say, helping you cook dinner, chatting with you in the car as you run errands, or even dropping by your office with you after hours so you can catch up on paperwork. Not only will she learn that beating egg whites makes them foamy, that it's fun to invent a rhyme pairing "car" with "far," or that Mommy goes to a specific place when she "disappears" to work every weekday morning, but she will also begin to accept the fact that hers is not the only important agenda and that a vast array of new adventures await her beyond the playroom.

LEARNING FROM OTHERS: A WORLD OF STIMULATION

If an infant focuses most intently on her own internal experience, and a one-year-old on her evolving relationship with those closest to her, the two-year-old gradually becomes open to expanding her social world beyond her immediate circle. This turning outward, stimulated in part by her growing awareness of her surroundings in general, is a slow, uneven process and requires a great deal of effort. Your toddler may peer curiously at the mailman as he stops by each day but quickly duck behind you if he so much as looks at her and says hello. This is not necessarily a sign of shyness, but more likely a symptom of your child's attempts to deal with what is still an overwhelming flood of new information. As she grows more familiar with the reassuring rules and common formulas of social interaction (as you show her how to say hello, announce her name when the mailman asks her for it, and so on), such interaction will cease to confuse her and she will begin to make contact with greater confidence.

Your child's fascination with other children will continue to intensify as well, drawing her more and more into social interactions. Just as when she was one, she learns a great deal by imitating her peers. Even when this acquired behavior is "bad" (hitting, snatching toys, yelling), it opens the door for exploration and discussion. By commenting on

Imitating peers and pretend play are two activities your two-year-old will engage in more than ever before.

what has happened ("Look how sad the boy is because he got pushed on the slide"), you help her understand that actions have natural consequences. As the months pass and your child interacts more with adults outside her family and with other children, her focus will move gradually from "me" to "me and sometimes you, too." Her ability to empathize will expand, and as her willingness to wait for what she wants gradually grows stronger, she will begin to share, take turns, and experiment with other social skills.

Your two-year-old's ability to interact with a wider world is largely a result of her greater general awareness of her surroundings. By age twenty-four months, a toddler is all eyes and ears, soaking up everything around her (good and bad) like a sponge. Her longer memory and increased comprehension help her retain and use what she takes in. As a result, she not only learns the social rules and ethical principles *you* teach her but experiments with the variations she observes in others. Now more than ever it's important to consider your child's presence when you are in conversation with other adults, when you are stressed emotionally or having an argument with your spouse, or when the television is on. Though it is neither possible nor desirable to screen everything that reaches your child, it is only considerate to protect her from information that is emotionally overwhelming or inappropriate.

THE TOY BOX
At Thirty Months

Ever since he was born, Richie has been a confirmed night owl, and his weary parents, Janet and Dave, soon fell into the habit of letting him play with his toys in the living room after dinner while they enjoyed their nightly TV programs with their two older sons. Tonight the family is watching the evening news, and they hardly notice Richie assembling his wooden train set behind an easy chair, talking quietly to himself. Just as Dave leaves to get something to eat in the kitchen, a story about a fatal plane crash in London comes on. "Dave, come here," Janet calls. "Your boss is in London right now, isn't she?"

As Dave returns, Janet feels Richie's hand on her knee for a moment, but she is too engrossed in the news story to pay attention. The two parents and their older sons watch the screen anxiously. Suddenly, Janet notices that Richie's hand is gone from her knee, and his play chatter has changed in some subtle way. Looking over at her son, she sees that he has crammed a small wooden giraffe and a monkey into one of the train cars. He picks up the car, hurls it through the air, and smashes it into the ground. "Boom! 'Splosion!" he announces.

Janet is startled. She had no idea that Richie was paying attention to the news story. Yet he has effortlessly picked up on its emotional content and its effect on his family. Janet stands up quickly. She knows that Richie is too young to comprehend exactly what he's saying, and she doesn't want to increase his interest in the subject by dwelling on it. Instead, she takes his hand and, with a pointed glance at her husband, says, "Come on, Richie, let's go find a book to read."

A PLACE AT THE TABLE: YOUR THIRTY-SIX-MONTH-OLD

It is amazing to consider how much information a two-year-old ingests over the course of a year, and how competent she becomes at mastering her steadily expanding world. As frustrating as it can be at times to deal with her determination to control events around her, and as draining as her constant questions and high activity level can be, you can't help but feel some awe at her sheer determination to perfect her skills and grow. In just twelve months—a year that slipped by for her parents in a mere instant—Amy has evolved from a single-minded toddler, focused on imposing her will, to a more confident, mature young individual with her own clear tastes and opinions, a better sense of verbal give-and-take, and a stronger (if still sporadic) desire to please her parents and to look at things from the point of view of others.

Amy's parents have grown this year as well, Maggie acknowledges to herself as she sits down to dinner with her family. She and Richard have learned to plan ahead to avoid unnecessary conflicts with their daughter. Their growing knowledge of her strong personality has helped them rearrange some of their family habits and customs in ways that ease stress at home. "Would you like a roll, Amy?" Maggie asks her daughter as the family passes around the bread basket. "Yes, please," Amy replies—polite as ever. Her father hands the basket to her, and Amy carefully chooses one for herself. This time the rolls have been buttered ahead of time. After Amy tears her roll open and takes a big bite, she passes the basket to her brother. "Here," she says. Maggie and Richard exchange an amused glance. Amy is just as passionate a little girl as she always was, but at least her passion is being directed in a positive way toward her dinner and not wasted in a tearful outburst.

Parenting a two-year-old is all about respecting a toddler's need to control her environment while leading her toward new experiences as she is ready for them. It's not easy to know when your child needs a gentle nudge and when it's time to step back. By observing your unique child—learning the signals she gives when she's beginning to feel overwhelmed, noticing when she's bored or restless, gauging her level of development from her day-to-day behavior—you can support her growth in positive, stimulating, nurturing ways. As you read in the chapters that follow more about how toddlers grow, compare the information I give you with your experience with your own child. How is your toddler different from the portraits I provide? How is she the same? Keep in mind that no child will exactly follow any blueprint put forth in books, including the developmental timetables in the following chapters, which are intended not as a "test" but as a rough guide. It is, after all, the vast inconsistencies in the ways children grow that keep them fascinating. Resist the temptation to push your child to perform every skill described in these pages, but use the information to inspire you to better observe and act on her behavior and to appreciate the fact that your toddler is different from all others. The seeds planted during her earlier years are about to blossom in your child. This is not the time to judge but to open your eyes and see.

KEEP IN MIND . . .
Parenting Concepts for the Third Year

In the rush, chaos, and onslaught of unexpected challenges that fill the lives of families with two-year-olds, it's easy to lose sight of the parenting goals you've created or the new approaches you've been meaning to try. Here you'll find a few general pointers to keep in mind as you guide your child through the months ahead. By considering these general guidelines with your partner and your child's other caregivers, you can start to create a working parenting plan, and improve your family's daily experience as a result.

THINK PREVENTION, MINIMIZE FRUSTRATION. Your two-year-old doesn't profit from repeated experiences of failure. Simplify her environment and avoid overwhelming situations so she will have more chances to succeed.

CHOOSE YOUR BATTLES—YOU CAN'T WIN THEM ALL. Make a list of the behaviors you want your child to change, and focus on only the top one or two at a time. Eventually, you will work your way all the way down the list, but don't expect too much too soon.

LET YOUR CHILD MAKE SOME CHOICES, TOO. Your child will be much less prone to tantrums and other acting-out behavior if she feels she has some control over how her day will go.

THINK SAFETY. Two-year-olds can climb higher, run faster, and get into more dangerous places than you think—yet they are not very aware of the physical dangers that surround them. Overestimate your child's physical abilities and underestimate her level of vigilance when looking out for her well-being.

TALK YOUR WAY THROUGH THE DAY. Two-year-olds soak up new words like sponges. Providing your child with new expressions and ideas stimulates her thinking and helps her manage her emotions better as time goes on.

SEE EVERY DAY AS A CHANCE TO LEARN. You don't have to actively teach your child for her to learn. Children learn from helping around the house, playing in their rooms, and chatting with you while riding in the car. Be aware of the potential for expanding your two-year-old's thinking with each new experience or encounter.

PROVIDE "LANDMARKS." Two-year-olds need to know that the people, places, and things with which they're familiar will be around to support them as they venture forth into the unknown world. By providing your child with predictable routines and offering her a favorite toy or your hand to hold in an unfamiliar situation, you will help her work up the courage to experience something new.

THINK "TODDLER": REMEMBER YOUR CHILD'S AGENDA. Just because you're late for work doesn't mean your child feels rushed. Just because you want to eat a restaurant meal in peace doesn't mean your child understands why she must sit down and stop playing with the silverware. Hard as it can be, consider what your child's needs and motivations are before judging her behavior.

FIRST-PERSON SINGULAR

The most effective tool in successfully parenting your child is your own observation of her particular personality and style. Take a moment now to consider what you know about her already. How is her personality expressed in her day-to-day behavior? Is she generally adventurous, sensitive, placid, or fearful? Is she happiest snuggled up with you, roughhousing with her brothers, attempting a new physical feat, or painting pictures or looking at books alone? Which of her behavior patterns do you find most unproductive, and which would you like to encourage this year? At what times or in what circumstances do the two of you fall into frustrating loops of negativity ("You will!" "I won't!") that you would prefer to avoid? By writing down your thoughts, ideas, and observations now, you can compare them to your feelings about your child twelve months hence—and ponder the ways in which your child's temperament, her environment, and your own expectations have brought the entire family through another year of growth.

READER'S NOTES

CHAPTER 2

Jump, Color, and Dance— My Physical Abilities

Your child is getting wiser in the ways of the physical universe and more realistic about his own limits.

It's Sunday afternoon, and Peter has taken twenty-four-month-old Jesse to the playground while his wife, Diane, catches up on some house-work. The weather is warm, and the playground is packed with chil-dren. Peter and Jesse have spent many afternoons here before, and after unbuckling Jesse from his stroller Peter automatically leads his son toward the fenced-off section for toddlers. This time, however, Jesse tugs eagerly on his father's hand. "No!" he says, and points to a tall slide nearby. "Go here."

"But, Jesse," Peter replies over the noise of shouting children, "this space is for the big kids. You could get hurt."

Jesse frowns, then snatches his hand away. "I slide!" he crows, rac-ing through the crowd to the slide's long metal ladder. As Peter hurries to catch up, Jesse climbs the ladder like a pro. Peter is impressed and wonders, *Has Diane been taking Jesse to this part of the playground?* Not wanting to "baby" Jesse, Peter hangs back a little as his two-year-old balances at the top of the slide, then swoops down with a happy shout.

Oblivious to a little bump at the bottom, Jesse leaps up and looks around excitedly. "Swing!" he says, running through an open gate to the older kids' swings area.

"Jess! Wait!" Peter tries to maneuver between the groups of children to reach his son. As he reaches the gate, one of the swings flies just over Jesse's head, barely missing him. "Jesse!" Peter takes a flying leap and yanks him out of harm's way.

Jesse is not grateful for the help. "I swing!" he shrieks, struggling to break free. "Jesse, stop right now," Peter snaps, hanging on tight while he catches his breath. Then he helps Jesse onto one of the swings and, after making sure his son knows how to hang on, starts pushing. *Was I wrong to let him play here?* Peter asks himself as Jesse swings higher and higher. *He seemed so confident on the slide. But I don't think he had any idea that the swing could have hit him in the head. Am I supposed to make him stay in the babies' area, even if he's sick of it?* Glumly, Peter ponders this dilemma and keeps pushing the swing, hardly hearing his son's shrieks of pleasure.

Peter would be relieved to know that, as the months pass, his two-year-old's cognitive growth and experience will gradually temper his reckless behavior. As he continues to experiment with movement in a variety of ways—leaping, dancing, pounding, painting, brushing, splashing, and undressing with great energy and enthusiasm—he will grow steadily wiser in the ways of the physical universe and more realistic about his own limits. An increasing awareness of his surroundings, from flying swings to speeding cars and angry dogs, will help him build a list of reliable safety rules. The parent's job this year, as his two-year-old focuses more on mastering skills than on apprehending danger, is to act as "spotter"—standing by to rescue him when he needs it, helping him learn to adopt safe habits ("Don't go near the swings without a grownup"), but allowing him to lead the way whenever possible in his journey of physical discovery.

This journey will involve an improvement in not only his gross-motor skills (running, climbing, squatting, spinning, jumping, and even somersaulting) but in the important finer workings of his hands as well. This is a wonderful year to introduce "busy books" that allow him to practice buttoning, zipping, threading, and other fine-motor skills, especially when he is confined to a car seat, stroller, or crib. Paper, crayons, and kids' scissors will create new opportunities for self-satisfaction as he happily "works" at his table, just like Mom or Dad, or "does homework" like an older sibling. In fact, his desire to be just like you and others he admires will motivate much of his physical activity. Similarly, his inability to satisfy that desire (whether he's prevented from doing so or is simply unable to) will lead to angry outbursts and even tantrums. As trying as his shrieks and tears can be, it isn't hard to understand what he's going through. Just think back to how you felt as a teenager when your parents forbade you to stay out as late as your friends (preventing you from imitating those you admired), or, as an adult, when you were learning to use your first computer program (and were frustrated by the difficulty of mastering a new skill). In the end, despite the two-year-old's frequent inability to control his emotions, it's impossible not to salute his sheer will to perfect his skills in the face of all the obstacles that his safety-minded caregivers place in his path.

THE TOY BOX
At Twenty-four Months

It's a holiday, and Annette is enjoying a morning at home with her six-year-old daughter Andrea and Carlos, who's just turned two. She lays out modeling clay, cookie cutters, and a rolling pin on the dining room table. Andrea immediately starts to work, rolling out the green clay and using a tree-shaped cutter to create a "giant forest." Carlos watches in fascination, then reaches for the cutter. "I do it!" he says.

"Andrea's using that one," Annette points out. "Here's a cat-shaped cutter for you, Carlos. We'll roll out the yellow clay. You can make some wildcats for the forest."

Annette helps her son roll out the clay, and for a while this diversion keeps Carlos happy. He grabs the cat-shaped cutter and smashes it down on the clay. "Careful," his mother warns. "Do it gently, like this." Annette tries to show him how to avoid smearing the clay, but Carlos grabs the cutter back. "I do it!" he says. He smashes the cutter down again, smearing it even worse than before. Frustrated, he looks at his sister's orderly collection of clay trees. "Gimme!" he yells, and this time successfully grabs the tree-shaped cutter out of her hand.

"Hey, quit!" Andrea protests, but before she can stop Carlos, he has smashed the cutter down on her forest, squashing her creation. "Mommy, he's ruining everything."

"Okay, okay, Carlos, that's enough." Annette picks Carlos up and removes him physically from the table. *I should have known better than to expect them to enjoy this activity together,* she tells herself. *Carlos still gets too frustrated when his hands don't work as well as his sister's.* "We'll make a separate place for you to work, okay?" she adds. "I know—you can make a *jungle!* I'll show you how to make the snakes, okay?"

Scowling, Carlos grudgingly follows her over to his toddler table. He still wants to do what Andrea can do. But snakes are even better than trees—and anyway, he still has the tree-shaped cutter tightly clutched in his little hand.

"LET ME GO!": EARLY MOTOR ACHIEVEMENTS

What a pleasure it is to observe how happy and comfortable your twenty-four-month-old has become with his active, hardworking body. Now that he moves more efficiently and is sturdier on his feet, he has become less preoccupied with each step he takes and can devote more of his attention to the fascinating world around him. At this age, he may walk up and down stairs by himself (although some children still feel more comfortable crawling or sliding down steps), thus gaining access to cabinets and rooms that he hadn't known were there. He may run to keep up with his siblings rather than remain helplessly behind when they race off down the sidewalk. His greater ease with his body has also allowed him to begin developing more nuanced types of movements—from cutting, drawing with a pencil, and playing with clay to riding a Big Wheel, doing a somersault, and dancing to rhythmic music. As a result, his optimism and ambition have increased enormously. He is determined to master new skills—on his own terms and according to his own schedule.

This is a year when it's especially easy to see how your child's physical skills help him learn more about the world around him. Yet his ability to manage his body has profoundly affected his cognitive growth from his very first months of life. From the moment he learned to roll over on his back, he began to choose some of the stimulating sights and human interactions he would encounter. Once he learned to sit up at around six months, he began to grasp every object within reach in order to explore it with all his senses. When he learned to crawl, his learning opportunities increased a thousandfold, and as he began walking at around twelve months, his explorations expanded vertically as well as horizontally. At the same time, the development of his fine-motor skills allowed him to learn new facts about the physical world. By feeding himself with a spoon he learned that "If I move it too fast, it spills." Pounding pegs with a hammer taught him that "If I hit it too hard, it falls all the way through the hole." Drawing with chalk or oversize crayons led to the discovery that "If I move my hand this way, the color goes there, too."

The feelings of power and satisfaction these discoveries provide continue to motivate your child to venture farther into the unknown. As we observe later in this chapter, his abilities are likely to improve sooner than you expect, and his urge to experiment physically will be hard for him to resist no matter what the consequences. Your best strategy, then, is to arrange his environment so that he can experience new movements and sensations without getting into too much trouble. On quiet streets, go ahead and let him run down the sidewalk, but stay close enough to take his hand before he reaches the intersection. Encourage him to climb the stepstool to help you hang a picture, but be ready to help him back down. Let him try to "write" a letter to Grandmom, but help him finish

By two and a half, a child can sit still long enough to concentrate on her fine-motor skills, such as cutting with child-safe scissors.

it when his hands get tired and he starts to feel overwhelmed. As you bolster his confidence in these small ways, your two-year-old will learn that the world is a manageable and interesting place—and the link between his physical and cognitive skills will strengthen even more.

A PARENT'S STORY
"Cut the Paper, Not the Curtains!"

"I have to admit, I'm one of those moms who watched my son grow older with a certain amount of regret," a colleague told me while observing my own sons at play nearby. "When he was a baby, it was pretty easy to contain him in a limited space or just pick him up when he got too hyper. Once he became a toddler, his activity level really wore me out—especially after he turned two.

"I remember when he first started using kids' scissors. He was two and a half and just got completely obsessed with them. He had a little desk next to our kitchen table, and every morning he would sit and cut up magazines while I puttered around the kitchen. At first I was grateful that he was sitting still for a while. Then I started noticing little slices in the bottom of the kitchen curtains. A few days later, I found some holes in the knees of his sweatpants. Pretty soon I figured out that practically every time I turned my back, Mike started cutting up everything in sight. Back when he was one, I could have just taken the scissors away and distracted him, knowing he'd forget about them pretty soon. Now he wouldn't forget, and he wouldn't surrender control so easily. He and I had to figure out some compromise.

"The next time I caught him cutting the curtains, I sat him on my lap to talk about it. I realized that he had this urge to practice his cutting skills. On the other hand, I 'needed' for him to stick to cutting paper. We decided to go to the art store at the mall and see if we could find something that would make us both happy. As it turned out, they had some kids' scissors designed to cut only paper—nothing else! Mike loved them, and walked out happy as could be. I was relieved to find a way to limit his behavior without squelching his energy."

"LET ME TRY!": MOVING FORWARD AT AGE TWO

If one word can describe a typical two-year-old, that word is indisputably "active." Your child will be constantly on the move this year and will insist on directing much of his own physical experimentation and activity. As the first months pass, he will begin to pride himself on his ability (or, at least, his attempts) to take off and perhaps even put on some of his clothes, build a tower of blocks, wash and dry his hands, and brush his teeth (with your help). He'll also learn to coordinate the movements of his wrists, fingers, and palms, enabling him to unscrew lids, turn knobs, and unwrap paper as well as draw and cut. Clearly, his increasingly active and experimental nature will keep you very busy and may even become overwhelming at times. As always, the best way to cope with your eager little experimenter is to plan ahead—by putting a mat on the playroom floor for leaping and somersaulting, placing interesting containers full of harmless items in cabinets within his reach (while moving potentially dangerous items higher up), and using a gate to keep him out of non-child-proofed rooms.

As he approaches age two and a half, your child will express his joy in movement through gleeful "catch me" games and, like Jesse, swinging and sliding sessions on the playground. He may enjoy learning to pedal a small tricycle at this time. He will experiment with walking on tiptoe and standing on one foot—though, interestingly, jumping in place will still take great effort and coordination. At around his third birthday, he'll probably grow more interested in drawing with chalk and crayons and can begin learning to hold a marker in the writing position. He may enjoy imitating your vertical and horizontal strokes on a piece of paper, completing simple puzzles with your help, and using plastic kids' scissors with your supervision.

By the end of the year, your child will have graduated from his uncertain toddling to the more assured gait of early childhood—and his physical confidence will increase accordingly. After months of trying out all kinds of movement variations, such as galloping and trotting, and multiple actions, such as throwing a ball while running or eating ice cream while walking, he will come to a new, deeply fulfilling understanding of how his body works. To his great satisfaction, he can now kick a ball where he wants it to go, hit a baseball if it's placed on a tee, imitate a note on the piano, and steer his tricycle around a neighborhood filled with fascinating new people, places, and ideas. Thanks largely to your support and encouragement, he can look forward to a future full of exciting sports, enjoyable games, and one-of-a-kind arts-and-crafts creations.

A Different Drummer

Young children's physical accomplishments are often readily visible to adults. Unfortunately, one often gives in to the temptation to compare one child's progress with another's, so your two-year-old's level of activity may cause you some anxiety this year. Whether your child strikes you as much more active than others his age (so that you wonder if he's hyperactive) or seems disturbingly sedentary and quiet (causing you to worry that he's not developing on schedule), take his natural temperament into account before judging him in this area. As two-year-olds grow, their physical natures assert themselves more and more clearly. For example, your very active child may be overstimulated by crowds and responds to a busy playground by running around shrieking or dumping a pile of sand on another child's head. (If this is the case, it's best to remain near him much of the time, perhaps keeping a soothing hand on his shoulder and moving him to a less stimulating area when he seems overwhelmed or likely to hurt another child.) Or, your generally passive two-year-old may just have a calm, observant nature. If he seems content to sit and watch rather than frustrated by an *inability* to master a task, he is probably fine. (He could benefit, however, when you bring activities *to* him and encourage him to join in sometimes. That way, his laissez-faire attitude doesn't keep him from tackling new skills.)

Keep in mind that normal activity levels can often seesaw wildly this year. (Just as we sometimes throw ourselves too enthusiastically into a new exercise routine and suffer aches and pains the next day, a two-year-old may overextend himself one day and feel cranky and exhausted the next.) It is also important to remember that young children pass through many phases, physical and otherwise, before their personalities finally gel. Your very active or rather passive child may behave completely differently three months from now. When observing him, be sure to consider his behavior over the course of many months, or even a year. Don't "type" him too soon, because he will certainly pick up on your judgment. Rather than matching your physical style or expectations, focus on working at a pace closer to his.

If you are truly concerned about his activity level, poll your neighbors, relatives, or other adults who know him for their opinions. Have they also wondered whether something is wrong? If they agree with your sense that your child is not developing normally, talk with his pediatrician before he turns three. A child who is properly assessed before his third birthday can be admitted into an early intervention program and thus has a better chance to profit from corrective therapy.

PRACTICE MAKES PERFECT: REFINING MOVEMENT SKILLS

"Russell, stop taking your shoes off," a weary parent scolded her two-year-old in his stroller as they ate lunch in the food court of a crowded mall. "I said *stop*," she repeated as he pulled off the other shoe just as she was tying the first one back on. Finally, at her wit's end, she snatched both shoes off the floor where her son had dropped them and stuffed them into the stroller basket. "Fine, then," she muttered, bundling up their food and throwing it in the trash. "If you can't keep your shoes on, we'll just go home. You can stay barefoot all day in your room for all I care."

As his mother marched off with him toward the exit, Russell twisted around in his stroller to give her a puzzled "What did *I* do?" look. It was obvious to anyone—even to his mother, no doubt, if she had stopped to consider the situation—that Russell hadn't meant to provoke. He had simply felt compelled to practice taking off his shoes, and his fascination with the resulting physical sensations overrode his less urgent need to attend to what she was saying. It is a simple fact of parenting that watching your child *acquire* such skills as crawling or walking is typically very exciting, but standing by as he *perfects* them—fine-tuning the muscles through constant imitation, experimentation, and repetition—can drive even the most patient caregiver up a wall. Your child is not only likely to remove a given item of clothing repeatedly once he learns how but may also learn to love opening and closing the refrigerator door even after you've asked him not to, and jumping off the next-to-last step of the staircase despite the many times you've told him it isn't safe. Despite appearances, however, he isn't flouting your rules out of anger or defiance in any of these cases. He's simply responding to the same kinds of developmental urges that once commanded him to pull himself to his feet and start to walk.

Constantly curtailing your child's experiments with movement prevents him from developing coordination and other motor skills he needs to work on. It is also likely to end in shrieks of protest, futile struggles, and mutual misunderstandings that can establish a negative pattern for years to come. Still, the fact remains that children must keep their clothes on (at least sometimes), refrigerator doors must stay closed, and little ankles must not get sprained. One of your greatest parenting challenges this year is to find a viable compromise between your child's need to practice a variety of movements (even apparently nonproductive ones) and your need to limit his activity level or at least redirect his energy.

One way to meet this challenge is to plan ahead for your two-year-old's need to move. By installing a swing set in the backyard, making sure he has access to age-appropriate play equipment at a public playground or park, and taking him for romps in outdoor areas free of cars, you allow him to try out his muscles in a wide variety of new and exciting ways. It's also a good idea, when possible, to set up one or more areas inside the house where your child can jump, roll, and climb. Certain chairs and sofas might serve as designated climbing areas. Cushions, a carpet, or a mat on the floor can prevent some bumps and bruises when you aren't there to spot him. A large cardboard box makes a fine tunnel or house. Elsewhere, a small table and chair just his size can provide a suitable place for him to practice such fine-motor skills as cutting, painting, and drawing. It isn't necessary to provide expensive equipment; a sheet of paper taped to a tabletop works as well as an easel, and old magazines are perfect for cutting. Maintain the thrill of novelty by rotating these objects now and then, or introducing an occasional new find. Music provides another kind of variety because it helps your child learn to move to the beat, explore his body through leaping, bouncing, jumping, and spinning, and experience the pleasure of singing along.

You can help your child move creatively during everyday activities as well. By assigning him regular chores, such as watering a plant or putting his empty cup in the sink, you introduce him to the satisfying experience of familiar, oft-repeated movements. He can develop new motor skills by helping you in your own work, too—tearing up lettuce leaves for a salad, pushing the "start" button on the dishwasher, using his toy broom to help you sweep, digging in his own flowerpot-sized garden while you transplant some shrubs, and even "organizing" a variety of important-looking objects you've loaned him from your desk. Participating in these grown-up activities will fill your child with pride even as they help him develop his motor skills.

Encouraging your child to use his body in as many ways as possible may not only cut down on less productive activity but also stabilize his sleep rhythms. Particularly when his sleep routine is in flux, physical activity can help him use up excess energy that would otherwise prevent him from falling asleep. (Of course, it's also important to watch out for times when he risks getting overtired and becomes unable to sleep for that reason.) Though it's true that even a well-exercised child may repeatedly pull off all his clothes, open and shut the dresser drawers, and resist bedtime, these activities are likely to become shorter-lived and less frequent as he finds more interesting ways to move.

Meanwhile, the key to weathering this type of activity is, again, to plan ahead for the kinds of situations you know are likely to happen. If your child hates being buckled into a car seat, be sure you bring along a tape of children's songs when it's time to do errands so he can at least exercise his lungs and kick his legs to the beat. If you know he is likely to climb the furniture during a visit to a friend's house or perform chemistry experiments with the condiments at a restaurant, don't forget to pack an activity book or paper, crayons, and stickers to keep him occupied. (Better yet, frequent restaurants that cater to kids—providing crackers to munch on and plastic cups with lids.) Some activities, such as Russell's shoe-removal experiment at the mall, are probably better off simply tolerated or ignored. By tossing the shoes in the stroller basket and letting her son just wear his socks, Russell's mom could have finished her lunch in peace. Likewise, a two-year-old who eases his boredom by repeatedly squatting and jumping up, squatting and jumping up while in line at the bank with Mom, is dealing with confinement as best he can—despite the disapproving looks of the adults around him.

Throughout this year, it's important to remember that your child does not yet know how to regulate his own activity level—he is not necessarily able to slow down when he is exhausted or when he sees that you are losing patience. Just as you "spot" him on the playground to protect him from harm, it's important to guard him from excesses in activity level as well—setting healthy limits and helping him channel his energy in ways that are productive, tolerable, and fun.

EASING THE WAY
Coping with Your Own Physical Limits

Given the fact that your two-year-old will need to keep moving in all kinds of ways, it's wise to consider your own level of energy and tolerance and to think of ways to cope during those times when you feel worn out. The good news this year is that your child is finally fully able to understand your words when you tell him to "stop that right now." The bad news is that he is still frequently *unable* to make himself stop on command, since brain and body don't always work effortlessly together at this age. The confusion caused by this apparent paradox is one of the reasons why two-year-olds tend to suffer abuse at the hands of their caregivers more than infants or older children.

For this reason if no other, anticipating your own limitations is just as important as accommodating your child's.

If you know you simply do not have the patience or energy to put up with a two-year-old's energy all day (and few people do), think now about introducing a few pinch hitters—by turning your child over to your partner at appointed times, arranging for play dates or playground sessions where he can expend his energy on his peers, or finding enough quality child care to allow you to recharge. If caregiving relief is not an option for you, consider the ways in which you could structure and pace your day with your two-year-old so that the two of you reach your breaking points less often. Take care not to plan too many errands for a day when you're together. Call up a friend for a grown-up chat and a chance to blow off steam. On those occasions when you're simply exhausted and your child isn't, put him in a bubble bath and take a break nearby with a magazine.

Interestingly, many parents find that the strain of their two-year-old's activity level affects them emotionally more than physically. All that movement leaves little opportunity for the cuddling that felt so good in the past. If you feel this way, make sure you take advantage of the quiet moments to get the hugs and kisses quotient you need while your child is open to the idea, or indulge in gentle tickle games instead. After all, you are only human. If a sign of affection from your child can help you cope with his more typical "running-away" behavior later, it's important for you to have it.

ON THE RUN: KEEPING YOUR CHILD SAFE

"I had to take Jay to the emergency room again," Rebecca, a former client, told me when I asked her how her weekend had gone. "This time he tried to jump to the bottom of an escalator. Four stitches in his

Since two-year-olds are more mobile and daring, parents need to be ever alert to potential dangers.

forehead." I could hear the dejection in Rebecca's voice, and no wonder. Just two months before, Jay had cut his leg badly while trying to climb a wrought-iron gate, requiring several stitches in his shin. "People must think I'm a terrible parent," Rebecca said in a low voice. "I try to watch him. He's just so active, I feel like I spend all my time running after him, yelling, 'Watch out!' "

Though it was true that Jay was an unusually active, adventurous toddler, nearly all two-year-olds prefer to be constantly on the move. Their eagerness to practice new skills—along with their ability to acquire these skills very quickly—often leaves parents a bit behind the curve, struggling to keep abreast of their child's latest achievements. Even your toddler's physical growth can take you unawares this year. Many a two-year-old has quietly grown past the maximum weight requirement for his car seat (and perhaps also loosened the straps dangerously after months of squirming and tampering) without his parents' knowledge. It's amazing how quickly your child can gain access to an out-of-reach cabinet or an upper-story windowsill. The danger potential is only increased by the fact that, at age two, children don't always pay attention to speeding cars, bicycles, dogs, and other hazards that you routinely avoid. Shouting "Look where you're going!" won't immediately improve this situation. Research has shown that children under age four are generally *unable* to screen out distracting stimuli or to direct their attention in an efficient way. Your child can sharpen his awareness only with time and experience.

Your child's safety is also threatened by the fact that new abilities are not always as obvious as they were the previous year. It's much easier to note that your toddler can crawl up a flight of stairs than that he has figured out how to twist the top off a bottle of cleanser. That is why it's important this year, more than ever, to *overestimate* your child's physical abilities and *underestimate* his level of experience and cognitive growth when safeguarding his environment. Even though your child hasn't yet shown much interest in jumping huge distances, for instance, and seems to acknowledge your commands to "stay with Mommy," it's still important to make sure you have a firm grip on his hand as you step onto an escalator. Even though he can't yet reach the knife drawer and has heard you warn him never to touch the knives, place them even farther out of his reach this year. He knows how to stand on tiptoe now, and he'll soon figure out how to move the stepstool. Even if he has never choked on his food, you will want to cut grapes in fourths and avoid giving him raw carrots, popcorn, hot dogs, lollipops, hard candies, and nuts. Though he has never tried to climb out of his car seat and now insists on buckling himself in, make sure you check to see that the buckle is properly closed. You never know when he will decide to start trying to climb into the front seat, and his ability to close a buckle isn't foolproof.

All in all, it is better for everyone if safety is considered ahead of time and becomes simply a part of family policy, rather than something you have to make a pronouncement about as each new situation arises. If a two-year-old is consistently told that he can't touch the iron because "that's the rule," he's less likely to try to grab it every time you start to iron your clothes (especially if you assign him an important job, such as separating the shirts to be ironed from the rest of the laundry). If your "no-candy-with-nuts" policy has been long in place owing to the danger of choking, he's used to candy without nuts and will be more likely to avoid it at friends' houses and elsewhere. Assessing your child's energy level should also become part of your family's safety routine. Note when he is becoming too exhausted to control his impulses, and point this out to him in understandable ways ("Okay, Geoffrey, you look beat. That's enough playing tag for now"). Suggest ways for him to change his pace before an accident happens ("Let's take a break. What book should we read?"). As time passes, your child will gradually learn to monitor his own activity level, becoming more vigilant and less "accident-prone."

A CHILD'S-EYE VIEW
Kickball

Ball! Two-year-old Mick spots his favorite red kickball in the corner of his room. He picks it up, enjoying the feel of it filling the space between his arms. *Roll.* He remembers how Daddy rolled it to him when they were "playing soccer" last week. He drops the ball now and throws his body on top of it. It rolls back and forth a little under his tummy. He giggles.

"Daaaaaddy!" Mick picks up the ball and wanders out of

his bedroom, looking for someone to play with. There's the sound of a television downstairs, but otherwise the house is silent. Mick goes to the top of the stairs and peers down. He looks at the ball in his hands. He looks at the stairs. *Roll down the stairs?* he wonders. Laboriously, he climbs down the first couple of steps, then places the ball on a step and gets ready to jump over it.

"Mick!" Daddy has appeared at the bottom of the stairs. "I told you not to play with the ball on the stairs!" He leaps up the stairs and grabs the ball, catching Mick just before he topples backward toward the floor. "We never, *ever* do that," his dad tells him firmly. "We play with balls *only* outside or on the flat floor."

Mick stares at his dad, stunned. *He took my ball away!* he thinks. A feeling of outrage overwhelms him. He starts to cry.

"It's okay," his dad tells him patiently. "I know you don't like it, but that's the rule. Come on outside. I'll show you how to kick the ball to me, and I'll kick it back."

Kick the ball. Mick looks outside. He looks at the ball. Making the connection, he remembers what fun he had last time playing ball with Dad. Still whimpering, he follows his dad outside. "Gimme the ball!" he yells. "I kick it!"

"THIS IS ME": GETTING TO KNOW THE BODY

It's a fact that every two-year-old loves his body—not just the many new ways it can help him get where he wants to go, but its textures, shapes, smells, and amazing, apparently infinite variety of sensations. This is an age when it's a burden to put up with layers of clothing that chafe sensitive skin, weigh down limbs that long to move freely, and muffle contact with the outside world. You are quite likely to find yourself devising all kinds of ways to convince your two-year-old to keep his diaper on, let you help him with his coat, put him in his bath, and take him out again. The upside of this extreme body consciousness is the joy of watching your child glory in his physicality—admiring his reflection in the mirror, shrieking with pleasure as he runs naked around the house, and gently caressing the different surfaces of his face, his hair, his tummy, and his feet.

Of course, the two-year-old's passionate exploration of what he has only recently come to understand is his separate, inviolable self also includes his genitals. If he hasn't already done so, he will no doubt soon discover that this area is not only intriguing to look at but fun to touch. This is a year when most children indulge at least occasionally in self-stimulation. They talk and even brag about their penis or vagina and become curious about what others' "private parts" look like. Though curiosity about the body is perfectly normal, it's also true that frequent self-exploration makes others uncomfortable and may eventually get in the way of your child's relationships. For these reasons, it's a good idea to de-emphasize such behavior, gently diverting your child's attention without making him feel overly inhibited or ashamed. (Remember that a dramatic response will only encourage him to test your reactions again.) Talk with him about the concept of privacy and the value of engaging in certain acts only when alone. If he seems unable to stop his self-stimulation, or if it continues at a very high level for many months, discuss the issue with your child's pediatrician. But if his interest is in the normal range, remember that his fascination with his body can lead to productive—or at least preparatory—discussions about how our bodies work, the differences between boys and girls, and the advantages of using the potty.

Q & A
"Stop That!"

Q: My two-year-old, Emma, has gotten into the habit of sticking her hand down her pants whenever she's just standing around. I've asked her to stop it, but she tells me, "It's warm down there," and, "It feels good." She seems to do it as unconsciously as other kids suck their thumb. Obviously, it's especially embarrassing for me when we're out in public. Is there any way I can get her to break this habit without making her feel ashamed of her body?

A: Unfortunately, when a habit is as frequent and unconscious as this one is, it can be difficult to break. However, your child does not seem emotionally obsessed by her private parts and in fact doesn't even seem to think about what she's doing very often. The more upset you act about this issue, the worse it will get. If she realizes that she can get your undivided attention by performing this act, she will do it more often and more aggressively. By talking to her casually—both when she's performing the act and when she isn't—about the need to keep "private parts" private ("Do you want to be by yourself?"), and quickly but calmly removing her hand when she does begin to touch herself ("Emma, where should your hand be?"), you will keep the focus on the habit and not its emotional dimension. Eventually, as she realizes that she wins your positive attention more easily when she's not engaged in this awkward habit, she will start to do it less often. Even without your help, she will probably outgrow it soon enough. Meanwhile, remind yourself that it is the rare two-year-old who does not experiment with this behavior, and that the time is approaching when she will become more interested in adapting to society's rules.

"I CAN DO IT, TOO!": LEARNING TO MOVE WITH OTHERS

Two-year-olds not only take great satisfaction in learning to control their bodies but also delight in an expanded array of experiences as their movement carries them out into the larger world. Their new ability to leap, climb, and dance and their increasing familiarity with creative pursuits such as cutting and drawing open the way to pleasurable social interaction with other children their age. This is a good year to begin encouraging friendships on the playground or in the neighborhood and teaching your child simple indoor and outdoor activities that are fun to do with other kids. (These include turn-taking games such as "Go Fish," matching games like "Concentration," ball-tossing games, bowling sets, and so on.) You might even consider enrolling your child in an early-childhood gymnastics, music, or other movement-related class. Much of the time, younger two-year-olds still resemble bumper cars as they move about a room, engaging in parallel play but not really interacting much. Still, as the year unfolds, your child will benefit from the opportunity to imitate and experiment with motor skills he sees other children engaged in.

Another advantage of moving with others is that it helps to make those movements conscious—to link the *idea* of a physical act in your child's mind with the way it *feels* as he makes it. This link can be strengthened by asking your child to watch other children or adults accomplish a movement and then mimic them, or by describing a movement as your child does it. Many movement-oriented songs and games aimed at toddlers and preschoolers ("Head and Shoulders, Knees and Toes," "The Hokey-Pokey") accomplish this task, as do adults when they comment on a child's performance ("Look at you twirling around!") and early-childhood movement instructors as they work with preschoolers ("Jump high on the trampoline! Jump high, David!"). Two-year-olds frequently initiate this process themselves, in fact, narrating their own actions throughout the day ("I jump this big"). This process of linking a movement with the mental picture of it and the verbal expression—of connecting mind and body—leads to better coordination and physical confidence and is a vital part of growing up.

Q & A
What a Bully!

Q: My two-and-a-half-year-old is big for his age. When he's put with a group of kids, he usually ends up playing with children older than himself, since he appears to be their age. Lots of times this leaves him trying to take part in activities that he's too young to tackle, like T-ball or tag. When I put him back with the littler kids, however, he tends to bump into them a lot and accidentally get in their way. The other day I heard a little girl call him a bully when he pushed past her in the sandbox. What should I do?

A: Your child doesn't sound like a bully, from your description. He just sounds big. It's important to realize that his larger size can make coordination tougher. He needs plenty of opportunities to imitate others, to play in active, even boisterous ways, and to run freely without the danger of hurting others. To ease his frustration when trying to imitate children who are older than he but the same size, look for activities that are similar to "big-kid" pursuits but easier to manage, such as a plastic Big Wheel instead of a tricycle, or a soccer ball instead of a baseball. (Keep in mind, however, that there will be times when he'll want to do only the big-kid activity.) To help him in his relations with physically smaller peers, try to arrange some play experiences for your son with children who have younger siblings. By pointing out ways in which the older child helps or avoids hurting his sibling, you can introduce your son to the idea of watching out for others. Finally, when he is playing with smaller children, stay nearby to help him play without hurting them. Remind him that "these kids are smaller than you." The reality is that, being only two, he won't always be able to keep others' needs in mind. (If you're worried about other parents labeling him, you might remind *them* that he's just a two-year-old.) Because of his age, some of the responsibility for watching out for others is still yours.

"WATCH ME, DAD!": LEARNING TO MANEUVER IN A BIG KIDS' WORLD

It's hard to believe a year has passed, but Jesse is now three, and Peter, his dad, can certainly see the difference in the way he looks and moves. Though he hasn't grown much taller over the past twelve months, Jesse has developed much more confidence in his movement. His posture is better, he begins an action with less hesitation, and he can easily alter his direction or movement midcourse. He moves better with other kids, too, Peter notices. Exchanges with his peers are less awkward now and more like the interactions of later childhood. In fact, Peter realizes with a start (and a certain amount of wistfulness), Jesse is a "big kid" now—like the children who so outpaced him last year with their shouting and constant movement on the playground.

Peter never takes Jesse to the babies' area now. Instead, he follows Jesse as he pedals his tricycle to the larger area and carefully parks the trike next to a park bench. Usually, Peter sits on the bench and watches his son plunge into the chaos of activity, enjoying the sight of Jesse making contact with others and joining in their games. Today Jesse is mostly interested in swinging from the climbing bars, and he has managed to convince an older girl to lift him up so he can reach them. Suddenly, however, the glint of sunlight on a swing catches his eye, and in an instant he has dropped from the bars and raced toward the big kids' swings area.

"Jesse!" Peter is on his feet in an instant—much more experienced now about which equipment poses a danger for his child. As he moves toward Jesse, he sees his son hesitate at the entrance to the swings. Jesse's face takes on a serious look—and Peter almost has to laugh, it's so obvious that Jesse is mentally reviewing the rule about the swings: *Never* go in the swings area alone.

Almost in spite of himself, Jesse slows his pace, looks around for his father, and waits for him to take his hand. Peter joins him, relieved to know that his child has learned to some degree to be more cautious. "Want me to push you, kid?" Peter asks as Jesse leads him in a wide arc around the row of flying swings toward an empty one at the end. This time Peter won't be the parent racing to rescue his child from danger. Jesse has become an active, if still junior, partner in the effort to take care of himself.

Fine- and Gross-Motor Achievements in the Third Year

Here are a scattering of behaviors that parents often see at these ages. If your child doesn't demonstrate them at the time indicated, don't be alarmed. Think of these as new territory he will probably visit soon.

24 MONTHS   May climb and descend stairs alone

Much sturdier on feet

Likes to dance

Can stack three or more blocks

May show preference for one hand

27 MONTHS   Loves to run and to play chase

May pedal a tricycle

Likes to walk up and down stairs

Likes to jump off of steps, walls, and other surfaces

May unscrew lids, turn knobs, and unwrap packages

30 MONTHS   Experiments with varied movements such as galloping and hopping

May be able to kick a ball in an intended direction

Likes to use chalk and crayons

May use kids' scissors

33 MONTHS   Capable of throwing a ball, eating an ice cream cone, or otherwise moving while walking

Begins to walk more like an adult, with heel-to-toe gait

May alternate feet when climbing stairs

May be able to hit a baseball off a tee

36 MONTHS   Can easily ride a tricycle on his own

Can complete a simple puzzle

Imitates vertical and horizontal strokes on paper

FIRST PERSON SINGULAR

Now while the issues of your child's third year of motor development are fresh in your mind, take some notes about his latest advances in learning to manage his body, ensure his own safety, and interact physically with his peers. What new skills is he developing? How is he refining the skills he already has? What is his physical style—adventurous and risk-taking, quiet and hesitant, methodical and determined? How are his physical experiences different from those described in this chapter? How are they the same?

If you have a photograph or videotape of your child at age eighteen months or so, look at it and write down some of the ways in which his physicality differs now. If possible, videotape him now—on the playground, in the backyard, with other children—so you can monitor his changes next year. These observations of your unique, actively growing child are one of your most valuable tools in getting to know him as an individual—and in helping you more effectively discern his needs, uncover any difficulties as early as possible, and lead him toward greater growth.

READER'S NOTES

_____

_____

_____

_____

_____

_____

_____

_____

_____

_____

_____

_____

_____

_____

_____

_____

_____

_____

_____

_____

_____

_____

_____

_____

_____

_____

_____

_____

_____

_____

_____

_____

_____

_____

_____

_____

_____

_____

_____

_____

_____

CHAPTER 3

Creating a World—My Cognitive Development

I t is often difficult for parents of two-year-olds to know when their children are "winging it" and when they truly understand what is going on around them.

Christmas has always been Deborah's favorite holiday, and she can hardly wait to experience it this year with Kaisha, her two-year-old daughter. Born in early December, Kaisha slept through most of her first Christmas Day. The next year, at age one, she still wasn't really aware of what was happening. Kaisha's speaking ability and general comprehension have now advanced so astoundingly, however, that Deborah is sure her daughter will understand the idea of Santa coming down the chimney and leaving wonderful gifts for her. In fact, Kaisha does pick up quickly on Deborah's excitement about the coming event. On weekends, when Deborah takes her daughter shopping for gifts, she explains the concept of gift-giving and informs Kaisha that she, too, will receive gifts from her family and from Santa. Later, in the evenings, as they wrap the gifts together, Deborah asks her daughter, "Who's coming on Christmas?" and Kaisha answers with an excited "Santa!" The closer they get to the holiday, the more Deborah talks about the "big day" to her daughter, and the more Kaisha mentions it in turn. At bedtime, when Deborah tells her how Santa will arrive in a sled with all his reindeer, bringing gifts for good little boys and girls, Kaisha squirms with glee.

Finally, Christmas morning arrives. Despite a late night spent putting together the tricycle and other treats that Santa has brought for Kaisha, Deborah is up early with video camera at hand, ready to capture Kaisha's expression on tape as she discovers the gifts under the tree. When Kaisha awakens, her grandmother lifts her out of her crib and lets her walk ahead to the living room for her grand entrance. Right on cue, Kaisha stumbles into the room, rubbing the sleep from her eyes, cute as a bug in her flannel pajamas. Deborah watches through the camera lens as her daughter surveys the shiny new toys surrounding the Christmas tree. She looks up at her mother with a puzzled expression. "Where Santa?" she asks.

It is often very difficult for the parents of two-year-olds to know when their children are "winging it"—trying to maneuver their way through their days through imitation, repetition, and sheer improvisation—and when they truly understand what is going on around them. At twenty-four months, Kaisha is able to mimic her mother's words ("Santa's coming!"). She can hold in her memory the sight of Santa sitting in the mall surrounded by gifts, and she can even connect that memory with the sight of gifts under the tree at home in a rudimentary way. But because her brain is still in the process of developing and growing, she has yet to make the cognitive leap beyond observation and imitation to true understanding. She isn't quite able to hold the Santa "storyline" in her mind in its entire sequence—to connect the separate facts into a logical whole.

Your child takes that leap, to a large degree, in this exciting third year of life as she moves from a one-year-old's first grappling with the concepts of language and symbolic thought to a more sophisticated ability to imagine, consider, and express herself in words and in play. The renowned child development theorist Jean Piaget described this change as exiting the *sensorimotor* stage, in which learning occurs through direct interaction with objects (banging two cups together makes a noise), and entering the *preoperational* phase, in which more complicated mental connections are made (the small cup fits inside the big one, but not vice versa). As your child learns to think in words and to connect one idea to another, she will begin to notice and think more about what's going on in her environment—from the conversations others are having about her to the fluctuating emotional climate in her family. She will become more fully aware that others don't necessarily know what she knows or see what she sees, and she will begin to adjust her behavior accordingly. A longer attention span and stronger memory will enable her to mull over the facts, feelings, verbal interchanges, and other experiences she has each day and to try to fit them together in a way that makes sense. If the conclusions she reaches are often incorrect (monsters lurk in her bedroom closet, and every adult female is a mommy), the fact that she has created them indicates an exciting growth in imagination and the beginnings of logical thought.

A PARENT'S STORY
Just the Facts

"You always read in parenting books about how important it is to talk to your child at a level they can understand," Beth, a parent and one of my adult college students, pointed out in class the other day. "I thought I was really on top of things when my two-and-a-half-year-old, Annie, started asking me 'who bringed her' to Mommy. I avoided all the technical birds-and-bees-type stuff, since it was over her head, and just told her something like, 'You were in Mommy's tummy, and you grew bigger and bigger till it was time for you to pop out.' She seemed fine with that explanation and even talked about it later when I showed her pictures of myself pregnant with her. But then the other day, when we were having lunch at a restaurant, she saw a pregnant woman walk by and started chattering away about the time when 'you swallowed me and put me in your tummy.'

"I had had no idea she'd misunderstood me that way. But the more I thought about it, the more I realized that it made perfect sense to assume that if she was in my tummy, I must have swallowed her. It just goes to show that you can't assume anything about what little kids understand. Next time she asks a 'big question,' I'll explain it to her in a few different ways."

A WORLD OF NEW IDEAS: NEUROLOGICAL ACHIEVEMENTS IN THE THIRD YEAR

If you are like most parents, one of the first things you did once your child was born was count all her fingers and toes and breathe a sigh of relief once you'd convinced yourself she was born "complete." In fact, however, scientists have been confirming over the years that infants enter this world far from fully formed, at least in the area of cognition. The neurons that make up the brain are loosely wired at birth. Some basic connections have been made through genetic inheritance and environmental stimulation in the womb, but the lion's share of brain development takes place in the three years after the child is born. As has been demonstrated more and more over the past decade, the quality and content of the child's early environment play a huge role in how her intelligence quotient (IQ) and emotional state develop over the long run.

Since birth, your child has been busily processing information in her environment, creating neuronal connections in her brain. At first, that information came to her more or less randomly—her hand happened to pass before her face, and she managed to put it in her mouth. A caregiver appeared and smiled at her, and different neuronal connections were made. Once she was able to sit unsupported at age six to nine months, however, she began to investigate more deliberately—manipulating objects, throwing them, and otherwise actively investigating their properties. Her physical development opened up a dramatic number of learning opportunities. As she learned to stand, walk, and reach higher and farther in her second year, she was able to explore more widely than ever.

By her second birthday, your child was adept at seeking out new stimulation for her still-growing brain. Veteran of countless forays into mysterious cabinets, over challenging furniture, around beckoning street corners, and through intriguing open doorways, she had long since become familiar with such physical concepts as up and down, empty and full, open and closed. Her understanding of sequence, or the passage of time, had also deepened through increased interaction with the world—she had learned to anticipate brief sequences of familiar events (such as bedtime following stories) and even to comprehend your promise that one event (a visit with Grandma) would follow another (a drive in the car).

Now, as she not only stands on her own two feet but runs, climbs, and leaps, and as she begins to use words to demand the experiences she wants and needs, she is ready to take an even more active part in her own education. She can ask questions ("Daddy come?"), test hypotheses ("Nana here?" when the doorbell rings), repeat experiments ("Do it again!"), and seek out new adventures ("Pet doggie, pweeeeze!") without having to be led. This ability to feed her intellect independently of others is quite intoxicating; as this year progresses, she will grow increasingly eager to explore the larger environment outside her home. She will enjoy walks with you, she will love to be set loose in a park or playground, and given enough reassurance that you are there to support her, she will be curious about the new people she meets. As her physical environment and everyday routines grow increasingly familiar, she will gradually become less anxious and fearful when minor changes occur. You will find that she is willing to stray a little farther from your side, and that she's beginning to understand and occasionally accept such concepts as "later" and "soon." Her increased mastery is likely to make child-care leave-takings and other routine separations easier. She will understand more fully that when you drop her off you will return for her, though she is likely to regress when routines are disrupted or her energy is at low ebb. Though she still learns most effectively in a warm, trusting atmosphere from someone she knows and loves, her more relaxed, independent attitude may allow her to begin learning from others outside her family.

By her third birthday, your little one will have traveled a very long distance from her first amazing encounters with the outside world. Her brain is now nearly fully formed physically (though its connections will certainly be reinforced by each new experience). As her learning continues, she will move through her world with ever-greater confidence and skill—and her confidence will in turn enable her to continue reaching out for more knowledge. This year, however, is when the core of her cognitive growth becomes fully formed. As far as we know now, the third year completes the most important successive period of brain development for a young child.

EASING THE WAY
The Learning Game

Veterans of years of schooling, we parents sometimes tend to believe that learning is hard work—even for a two-year-old. In fact, however, young children learn best in natural, joyful interactions with those to whom they feel emotionally close. One of the easiest ways for your child to begin to familiarize herself with such concepts as counting, recognizing letters, and cause and effect—and to learn some of the many elements of social interaction, such as taking turns, sharing, following rules, and learning to win and lose—is by playing games.

Even before age two, your child probably loved such simple games as peekaboo and "This Little Piggy Went to Market." As her ability to imagine expands this year, she may create games with you that help her explore different sequences. Say, for example, that she pretends to whisper a secret to Mom, and Dad happens to respond by laughing loudly. His laughing causes mother and child to crack up, and the pleasure your child takes in this may motivate her to play the "game" again. By whispering to Mom again, she sets in motion the spontaneous "rule" that Dad will laugh. Such improvisational interaction is not only fun but helps your child explore the concepts of taking turns, cause and effect, modulation of voice, and sequence, and no one ever has to mention the word "rules."

More formal games can stimulate the minds of older two-year-olds, too, so keep an eye out for opportunities to try some. Even the simplest board or card games require players to take turns, share the spotlight, and learn how to win and lose gracefully (though, of course, she won't like losing and will have to struggle with her feelings about it). Such games also work well as a bridge between concrete and mental reasoning. (It is easier to understand the idea of "three," for instance, if she moves her marker three spaces on a board.) Your child will need your help in dealing picture cards, spinning the spinner, or matching the dominoes, but these minor challenges won't dim her enthusiasm for learning to negotiate new forms of stimulating play. Meanwhile, you can use her performance as a way of observing her mental progress. It is gratifying to see what great leaps in comprehension your child makes between one session of tic-tac-toe and the next.

"TELL ME A STORY!": THE DEVELOPMENT OF SYMBOLIC INTELLIGENCE

"I love books, and I've been reading to my daughter since before she was born," a neighbor said to me the other day. "When she was a baby, I read board books to her while she chewed the pages. When she got bigger, I let her tear up the pages and draw all over them as long as she'd let me read her another story. Frankly, I didn't care much if she was paying attention. I just liked the closeness of her sitting on my lap.

"But something's changed this past year, since she turned two. Now she actually brings books to me, and she gets mad if I have to stop before the end. It's like she actually wants to know what *happens* in the story. And she cares about the characters. She looks really sad when the kittens' mittens get lost, and scared when Hansel gets locked up by the witch. I wish I knew what happened in that little brain of hers to change her attitude toward stories. It's like she just started to *get it* all of a sudden. Is it because I read to her so much to begin with, or is it just part of growing up?"

My neighbor was right to be intrigued, and correct in her observation that her child's quality of attention was changing in important ways as she grew older. Nearly every infant loves to sit on her mother's lap and look at a picture book as Mom or Dad reads aloud, but not because she understands what her parent is saying. The ability to hold a sequence of mental images in the mind—to comprehend a story or even think about an object that isn't physically present—is extremely complex and will deepen tremendously this year. As this ability begins to supplement your child's sensory experiences, it will account for much of her mental progress in the future.

The roots of symbolic thinking reach deep into infancy. One of the earliest steps in learning to visualize an object is understanding the concept of *object permanence*—the idea that an object exists even when it is out of sight. As with many other aspects of babies' cognitive development, the age at which children are believed to comprehend object permanence has been repeatedly pushed back (mainly owing to more sophisticated tests devised by child development researchers) and is now believed to be around six months. Before this time, your baby was probably content to be left with a caregiver while you left the room. Once you were gone, her mind was fully occupied with the person who had taken your place. She couldn't really "miss" you because she couldn't picture you—she didn't understand that you continued to exist. Sometime between six months and one year, however, she began to realize that, though you went out the door, you were just on the other side of it, and her howls of frustration communicated her desire to join you.

Another major development in your child's thinking occurred around her first birthday, when she first began to sense that your thoughts were separate from her own, and that the two of you didn't always know what went on in each other's minds. As this awareness took root, she became increasingly curious about your responses to her actions and, in particular, your emotional state. Her experiments in this area—throwing her breakfast on the floor, for instance, to see how you'd react—evidenced her first real attempts to "think" about you as a separate entity; to predict, or picture in her mind what you might do next; and to figure out how she might influence you.

Next, at around eighteen months, great leaps in cognitive, verbal, and emotional development came together to allow her to begin to think in terms of symbols such as words, pictures, and ideas. By furnishing her mental world with spatial and time-related "landmarks," she developed the ability to picture the physical layout of a familiar room and to recall and predict a brief sequence of events. These first experiences of connecting ideas in a logical sequence, combined with a steadily lengthening memory, enabled her to plan ahead to some degree, to carry out her plans, to solve simple problems, and to engage in imaginary play. Still, most of her thoughts remained disconnected as she approached her second birthday—they more often resembled a series of still photographs than a continuously flowing movie. Missing the connections between one moment and the next, she could not yet follow a very complex chain of reasoning or hold a continuous storyline in her mind. If you lose your keys, you retrace your steps until you find them, but your eighteen-month-old was not yet able to think in this systematic way. She would look everywhere for the keys (even in places she hadn't been) or look past them when they were right in front of her.

The gradual development of symbolic thinking will continue throughout your child's third year, contributing more depth and shading to her thought processes. As the months pass, she will understand more fully that ideas and words can take the place of concrete experience, both within her own mind and when communicating with others. Child development researcher John Flavell of the University of Califor-

Everyday activities such as painting help a two-year-old's developing brain to thrive while she has fun.

nia at Los Angeles came up with a way to illustrate this change in perspective by showing a toy to young children and then asking them to tell their mothers (who were in an adjoining room) about the toy. Children closer to twenty-four months of age insisted that their mothers come and look at the toy while they described it. Apparently, they believed that their mothers had to see and touch the object to know it was there. Those approaching age three, on the other hand, were comfortable simply telling their mothers about the toy. They knew that she could picture and understand it through their words alone.

Your child's ability to rely less on direct experience and more on symbolic thinking depends on a number of underlying skills, including a decreasing level of *centration*. Centration (as in "concentration") is the tendency to focus on only one aspect of an object or situation—such as the color of a block (but not the shape), or the speed of a car (but not the color). If you and your twenty-four-month-old are playing with blocks on the floor and you ask her for the "yellow circle," she'll hand you the first yellow block she sees. As she moves closer to her third birthday, however, she becomes able to attend to an object long enough to notice more of its qualities. She may start to hand you just any yellow block but will then self-correct—putting down that block and finding the yellow round one. Another sign that she is noticing more aspects of objects is her intense need to correct imperfections in objects. You may *think* she won't notice a ripped page, a missing puzzle piece, or a broken toy—but be prepared to fix them!

Soon your child's awareness will expand to other aspects of her environment. She will notice details—sounds, images, qualities of objects, and small events—that you hardly notice or think about yourself anymore ("Mommy, listen! Airplane!"). Two-year-olds, with their brand-new ability to attend to the world around them, constantly surprise us with such comments as, "I go out through the squeaky door" (at the child-care center), or, "There's Billy! He has a green hat" (if he had one when she saw him last week). Her awareness of such details is a necessary aspect of symbolic thinking.

Another skill that supports symbolic thinking is *spatial representation,* or the ability to see things in the mind's eye. As experience with objects and people in her environment continues to create and fortify neuronal connections in your child's brain, she will be able to hold and manipulate an image or idea in her mind without relying on physical contact. Clearly, your child can think or talk about an absent object (the block tower she built) or a series of events (yesterday's trip to the ice cream shop) only if she can picture them in her mind. A lengthening attention span supports this ability, and all three skills come together to strengthen your child's memory—resulting in a new ability to reason and maintain longer trains of thought.

As with any skill, the more your child practices thinking symbolically, the better at it she will become. You can help her develop her ability to make mental pictures by using as many visually descriptive words as possible when pointing out an object ("Look at the bright red truck!") or commenting on the pictures in books ("See the big cow? What noise does a big cow make? MOOOO!"). Once your child begins to give you verbal reports of her own, be sure to ask for visual details

("What color was the ball?" "Was the boy big or little?"). By referring frequently to objects that aren't present, and to events after they have been completed, you can stimulate her memory. Review your child's daily routines with her, asking, "I forget—what happens after bath-time?" and help her visualize her local geography with such questions as, "Where are those steps?" Of course, you know that she knows the answer to the question, but asking it lets her practice symbolic think-ing and gives her the experience of solving a problem successfully. Such exercises increase the kind of self-confidence that has been shown to lead to long-term success, both in and out of school. Even in preschool, teachers can see a very clear difference between children who have been encouraged to figure things out, solving problems on their own, and children who have not been encouraged in this way. A history of find-ing things or fixing things for Mommy and Daddy offers not only cog-nitive benefits, in other words, but emotional ones as well.

As your child approaches her third birthday, she will be able to solve increasingly complex problems, make more elaborate plans, and express herself more fully with words. Her ability to comprehend story-lines and to create very short "stories" of her own ("We went to the zoo and saw a big deer! I feeded him") will increase as well. A few well-placed words from you whenever the opportunity arises will help her imagination take fire—enhancing her experience as she begins chatting contentedly with her dolls, building roads for her trucks out of blocks, and solemnly "purchasing" items at her cardboard-box grocery store. The development of her ability to reason and communicate will be a thrill to witness—just one reward for a year of active, involved conver-sation and play.

THE TOY BOX
At Twenty-six Months

It's snowing today, and David's mom, Frieda, has announced that the wind is too cold to venture outside. She lets him watch a children's TV show while she catches up on the bills, but after fifteen minutes he wanders back to her desk in search of some other distraction. "I know," Frieda says. "Let's look in your toy basket. I'll bet there's stuff in there that we've forgotten all about."

As snow falls outside, Frieda and David go through the toys in the basket that she keeps near her desk. David pulls out a fuzzy puppet. "Look!" he says, as delighted as if the toy were brand-new. "Fwoggy puppet!"

"Right!" Frieda says with a big smile. "That's the puppet Grandma gave you for your birthday, remember?" She puts it on her hand. "Remember how Grandma said, 'Ribbit,' in that creaky voice? She sounded so funny, didn't she?"

David laughs. "Wibbet!" he says, sounding just like Grandma.

His mother smiles and swoops the puppet down toward his face, but David is already digging again in the toy basket. He pulls out a busy book and hurries to undo the buttons on the cloth cover before his mother can help him. "My book," he says with satisfaction.

"Right," Frieda agrees. "Those are pretty buttons, huh? Red and yellow and blue." She turns back to the bills, giving him time to himself, but glances over a few moments later and adds, "Look, one button is round, like Mommy's eyes, one's square, and one is a triangle. All different shapes. What else is in that book?"

As David turns the cloth page and chatters on his own, Frieda returns to her work with satisfaction. Though David's use of words and other symbolic tools is still quite limited, she knows that he understands much more than he can say. In the meantime, she has helped him practice creating images in his mind by stimulating memories, describing objects' visual qualities, and comparing similar objects to one another. Now he's off on his own, elaborating on what he sees in his own developing imagination. *Not bad for a snow day,* she tells herself.

"I TRY NOW!": FROM IMITATION TO SELF-EXPRESSION

From the very first time she smiled, your little one has been a master of the art of imitation. Responding to instinctive urges, she has learned to clap her hands, say her name, feed herself, and walk and talk in much the way that you do. Clearly, she does not imitate just because it's fun. It's also a way to attract positive responses from the people she loves, to enjoy the feeling of "being just like you," to experiment with new, intriguing behaviors (as when she smashes a tower of blocks just after watching another child do so), and to learn and perfect a new skill.

From the beginning, imitation has formed the basis of learning for your child. The process of actually performing an action seems to forge deeper connections in the brain, making it easier for a very young person to recall that connection later. A study of sixteen- to twenty-nine-month-olds by Canadian researcher Leon Kuczynski and his colleagues at the National Institute of Mental Health demonstrated that a major change takes place in this type of imitation during the third year. Younger two-year-olds tend immediately to imitate an action they observe. Children nearer age three do so less often and instead re-create the action on their own a few days later. Clearly, a better memory and an improved ability to visualize actions in their minds support this change.

As your child's capabilities improve, she begins to move away from simple imitation toward *elaborating* on others' actions and her own ideas. You are likely to encounter many examples of this process every day of your two-year-old's life. If the two of you spend the morning making cookies, for example—indulging in little tastes of the cookie dough as you drop it onto the baking sheets—she's likely to elaborate on that experience by rolling out and "tasting" a piece of modeling clay that afternoon. By the middle of the year, she may begin to elaborate on ideas as well. She may respond to a friend's refusal to play by trying one ploy after another to convince him to participate, and if he won't, she may come up with more than one explanation ("Jon-Jon's tired") for his refusal.

Elaboration is a vital step in the two-year-old's process of moving beyond immediate, concrete experience toward more complex thought, and it should be encouraged whenever possible. You can reinforce your child's ability to elaborate by noting when she is beginning to run out of ideas in her play and supplying a new variation or two ("Look! Froggy's sorry he hit your doll. He's giving her a kiss"). The idea is not to *direct* your child's improvisation but to follow and support it, lending a helping hand over the difficult spots. "Post Office" is a good game for encouraging this process. Early this year, you might suggest that your child scribble a pretend letter, then help her fold it, put it in an envelope, and pretend to mail it in a mailbox. As she grows older, your child might prefer to dictate a letter while you write it. (If you always add, "I love you," at the end, she will learn to read the phrase eventually.) By the end of the year, you could start the game with, "Let's write a letter about your new kitty," or, "Let's send Nana a letter so she'll be surprised." Such elaborations help her build on a solid base of earlier knowledge and lead to increasingly higher-level thought.

By the middle of her third year, your child will probably be quite adept at elaborating on previous ideas and playing with new solutions. As a result, she will start to enjoy such problem-solving exercises as taking apart toys and trying to put them together, working simple jigsaw puzzles, and participating in creating daily routines and resolving conflicts between the two of you. Her developing symbolic thinking will also help her move from simple logic toward the beginnings of creativity.

One of the cognitive skills required for this new creativity is the ability to compare a model of an object to the real thing. Only when this is possible can a child draw a picture of her dog, for example, or guess what you are drawing before you finish it. Researcher Judy S. DeLoache of the University of Illinois has found that this ability to construct models forms quite abruptly, generally between thirty and thirty-six months. She demonstrated this through a study in which children were asked to find an object hidden in a room. Once they had done so, they were asked to find a miniature version of the object in a miniature scale model of the first room. Very few of the children aged two and a half or younger could make the connection between the room and the model, but nearly all the three-year-olds could. Clearly, this new understanding that one thing can stand for another not only enhances your child's drawing ability but enables her to think more flexibly, make more complex comparisons, and solve problems more creatively.

You can observe how your child's symbolic intelligence is expanding by comparing her drawings over a period of several months. As her ability to work with mental concepts increases, her drawings will become more symbolic. Between ages one and two, she may like to scribble but will probably not try to draw a recognizable object (though she'll label a picture a "cat" or "dog" if you ask her to). By the time she is approaching her third birthday, however, she may create pictures that look something like animals or people. Harvard University psychologist Jerome Kagan constructed a study to demonstrate this development. Children were asked to copy the examiner's drawing of a face. At sixteen months they produced just a scribble, at twenty months a rough circle, and at age two a better circle. By thirty months, however, most children attempted to place a few dots or lines inside the circle to represent parts of the face. The ability to "model" reality had asserted itself.

Following your child's progress in learning to solve problems and create story sequences can teach you a great deal about how far she has come in her ability to understand and analyze her environment. Not only is playing with a two-year-old lots of fun, but it offers new ways to share and compare views about each other and the rest of your world. Drawing a picture for your child and asking her to identify what it is, mixing colors and commenting on the results, putting together a puzzle, and exchanging little stories and memories, all encourage her brand-new feelings of self-awareness, confirm the importance of her opinions, and provide you with insights you might not otherwise have had.

Too Much Video?

Q: My two-and-a-half-year-old has always been strongly attracted to television. She tries to turn it on practically every chance she gets. My brother gave her some computer software for toddlers recently, and now I can hardly get her to stop playing computer games. She's learned quite a few vocabulary words from both TV and the computer, and she can manipulate the computer mouse like a pro. But I wonder if she really benefits from these experiences, or if they might actually impair her development. I worry that sitting around watching TV will keep her from being a creative person later on.

A: If anyone ever doubted that children are born imitators, he has only to watch a two-year-old speak in the exact intonations of the characters in her favorite cartoon show. As two-year-olds' attention spans lengthen, they are able to spend more time actually drinking in every detail of the shows they watch and picking up every nuance of the interactions on the screen. Clearly, the content of these shows is of paramount importance, as is your presence to help interpret what your child sees. Some programs especially designed for children this age may actually stimulate her brain, especially if they reinforce what she's already doing at home (singing the ABCs, talking about sharing). Still, the essential passivity of television viewing renders it clearly inferior to direct, person-to-person interaction.

Educational computer software designed for toddlers is, in my opinion, a more valuable tool than TV or videotapes in helping two-year-olds learn to think symbolically, model reality, and practice their emerging mental skills. The best games allow children to manipulate "objects" or control events in ways that they can't yet manage in real life (completing a puzzle onscreen with a simple click, for example, months before they're able to fit pieces into a three-dimensional frame). Such experiences give children a sense of power and control—a very satisfying experience for any two-year-old. The interactive quality of computers keeps children's brains active. Well-made software adjusts itself to your child's ability, giving her plenty of chances to try again. Many games combine music, words, and visual images that tap into different abilities in the brain. Again, though, it is important to remember that nothing replaces real life in developing creativity, and computer time should be reasonably limited this year.

If you have a computer, think of the time you and your child spend with it as similar to storytime—that is, as a chance to sit close together and focus on the same activity. Make a point of playing the games *with* your child, talking with her about what she's learning, and drawing parallels from the ideas in the software to experiences in everyday life. Remember, the goal is for your child to have fun while learning, and the best games for this age are ones that don't have right or wrong answers but introduce concepts such as colors, shapes, and numbers, feature familiar objects, and adjust to your child's level of comprehension.

"I'M A DOGGY!": EXPLORING THE IMAGINATION

"I wonder sometimes what I did to make Miya want so badly to be something—anything—other than a little kid," Alisa, one of the members of my mothers-of-twins club, admitted to the rest of us the other day. "It seems like every morning when she wakes up, she's become a different animal or character in her mind, and if I can't guess from her behavior who she is, she won't have anything to do with me! This week, she was a puppy for two days, then Supergirl for most of the third day, and she spent the rest of the time being the horse she rode at the carnival last month. When we go out and people say hello to her, she answers them with barks or neighs or orders to 'Stand back!' Sometimes she's so into her game that she refuses to play with other children unless they play her way. I know preschoolers really get into their imaginations, but frankly I'm starting to wonder if she's going overboard."

As evidenced by the storm of anecdotes that Alisa's comment provoked at our meeting that night, parents often wonder exactly what goes on in the brain of a child who is deeply involved in imaginative play. They may worry, as Alisa did, that a child's desire to pretend means she isn't happy with the real world around her. They may see their two-year-old's interest in creating imaginary conversations as a retreat from the real human beings in her environment. Or they may suspect that their child insists on "being a horsie" as a means of wielding control. In fact, however, while any or all of these possibilities may play a minor role in your child's imaginary play, learning to pretend is a normal and vital step in a two-year-old's development—one that enables her to practice new skills, explore new concepts, and work out her anxieties and other emotions in a safe, productive way.

Even as an infant, your child used play to learn more about her world, moving more or less steadily forward in her explorations. Late in her first year, she considered a rubber ball something to squeeze and throw, and a bottle something to hold and put to her mouth. At age one, she began experimenting with more elaborate ideas—putting objects in contact with one another (a pot and a lid) and, by the end of the year, using toys as though they were real (pushing a toy car along the floor). By her second birthday, she was probably able to invent new and original uses for the objects she came across. She may have pretended to eat a ball as though it were an apple, to wear a cup like a hat, or to treat a plate like a table. *Animism*—her conviction that inanimate objects are alive—manifests itself at about this time. This is the year when you can make her food whimper, "Please eat me," and, wide-eyed, she'll do it. Soon her increasing ability to think symbolically will allow her to create simple metaphors—treating two balls of different sizes as if they were a parent and child—and to follow sequences of pretend actions with some imaginary elements, such as pretending to pour tea into a cup and drinking it. As she gets better at experimenting with a wide variety of "what-ifs," she may well become fascinated with exploring how it feels to "be" a puppy, her baby brother, her doctor, or even you for hours or days at a time. As her third birthday approaches, your child's increasingly complex thinking will allow her to direct scenes in her play rather than just physically interact with her toys. She may put a bottle to a doll's mouth, for example, rather than to her own. By her third birthday, she'll be such an experienced hand at pretend play that she'll be able to switch easily back and forth between imaginary scenarios and real ones. Now that she's a pro at pretending, she can *use* her imaginary play as a way to engage you in her activity ("You be the doctor, Mommy"), connect to other children, or consciously work out the answers to questions she's been pondering.

A 1994 study by Paul Harris and his colleagues at Oxford University illustrates how far two-year-olds progress in their ability to pretend. In the study, twenty-four-month-old children watched an adult pour pretend tea into a teapot and feed it to a stuffed animal. When the researcher asked what had happened, the children would talk about the animal getting "wet"—demonstrating that they accepted the pretend play as real. If the researchers tried to switch back and forth between the pretend reality and the real one, however (saying, for example, "How can he be wet? There's not really any tea"), the children would become annoyed and walk away. Clearly, holding the fiction and the reality in their heads at the same time was too overwhelming at this age. By thirty-six months, though, the children easily switched back and forth between the two, referring to the animal as real or stuffed, and the teapot as full or empty, depending on the context of the conversation. Unlike the two-year-olds, they were also able to elaborate on their play (saying the animal was sad because it had gotten wet) and to backtrack in the storyline (guessing that the animal had gotten tea poured on it when the researcher said it was wet).

In short, the quality of your child's play will be very different at the end of this year from what it was at the beginning. Yet its purpose remains the same. Whether she is banging a pot with a spoon to see what noise it makes, talking to her stuffed rabbit, or putting on Mommy's shoes to see what it's like to be a mom, your child is using play to expand on her experience—to learn more about her environment, herself, and others than she ever could in the real world. Clearly, this is a healthy and necessary process, best directed by your child herself. Just as you followed her lead when she crept around the house on hands and knees, it's best to follow her lead now in deciding what to use in her imaginary play, offering occasional suggestions to enhance the play she is already engaged in. To this end, make a point of providing an array of toys from which your child can choose. Variety is more important than quantity—she needs something to bang on or thrash about, something to share, and something to challenge the mind, but she doesn't necessarily need to have a dozen of each of these available to her every day. Once she has settled on a particular toy or activity (beads and string, for example), watch her experiment on her own, and when you see her attention start to flag or frustration building up, offer a couple of ideas to keep her imagination flowing ("What a beautiful necklace! Do you think your teddy bear might want to wear it? Look, I think he likes it").

Imaginary play cannot and should not be relegated solely to playtime. Imaginative thought and discussion can be introduced into nearly all the activities that fill your child's day—including chores, drives in the car, visits with relatives, and so on. The more effort you put into stimulating your two-year-old's thinking ("Look at that cloud. It looks like a sailboat"), the more actively and imaginatively she will stimulate her own mind as she grows older—and the more enjoyable she will be to have around.

A CHILD'S EYE VIEW
"Want Cereal?"

Buttah, cereal, popcorn . . . thirty-month-old Reed solemnly loads a selection of pretend groceries from his cardboard grocery store into his miniature shopping cart. He loves to "go shopping" at the little store he and Mom made together. It's fun to pick out the boxes and cans he recognizes from real life, and loading them into the cart makes him feel important and grown-up.

Today, however, there's a glitch in his usual play scenario. His teenage brother, Steve, sits slumped on the couch watching TV, oblivious to Reed's vital activity. *Soup* . . . Reed glances over at Steve again. *Why doesn't he watch me?* he wonders. Finally, having finished his shopping, Reed wheels his cart over to his brother and holds up an empty box of cornflakes. "Want cereal?" he asks.

"Huh?" Steve glances quickly at Reed, then back at the television. "Uh, sure," he says without looking at his brother. "Hand it over."

Reed ceremoniously places the box in Steve's hand. But Steve, not paying attention, drops the box. "Uh-oh!" Reed cries. "Cereal spilled!"

Steve glances at his brother and laughs. "That's okay," he says, picking up the box. "It isn't real anyway, right?"

As Steve starts watching TV again, Reed stands rooted in one place, frowning. *Looks like my cereal box,* he thinks. *When my box spills, we say uh-oh. Why won't Steve play with me?* He can't make any sense of his brother's comment. Frustrated, he grabs the cereal box out of Steve's hand, puts it back in the grocery cart, and marches out of the room. *Maybe Mommy will play store,* he tells himself.

IS IT TIME FOR SCHOOL?: LEARNING FROM OTHER CHILDREN

As your child learns to sing the alphabet song, grows curious about simple number concepts, and improves her ability to connect one thought to the next, it becomes easier to think of her as capable of

Note the incredible focus on this two-year-old's face as he experiments with concepts such as balance and weight.

learning much more about the world in which she lives. Though learning to recognize and name letters, write her name, or count beyond ten is not something every child is interested in (or ready for) at this age, there is much she *can* comprehend in the areas of social interaction, emotional self-mastery, rules and routines, the physical properties of objects, and her own physical abilities and limitations. Since imitation plays such a large role in learning under age three, and since children this age particularly enjoy copying their peers, a group education or care situation becomes a more intriguing prospect this year. In fact, an increasing number of parents (33 percent, according to a recent *Newsweek* poll) are deciding to enroll their child in preschool by age three—partly for reasons relating to child care or their jobs, no doubt, but also owing to a wider understanding of the benefits of a stimulating environment early on.

Certainly, a high-quality facility whose staff is well trained in early childhood development can provide a variety of new experiences for your child. She will have the chance to experiment with materials and specially designed equipment too expensive or messy for you to provide at home. Many children welcome the chance to interact regularly with others their age. Others enjoy a closeness with new adults that widens their view of the world. Any group care situation will allow your child to compare children's behavior patterns and adults' caregiving styles to what she has observed at home—giving you the chance to discuss such behaviors with her. She will also gain experience in learning to share, to take turns, and to cooperate—all very difficult skills that can be accomplished only with practice.

Nevertheless, group education is not the best choice for every two-year-old. As in most other aspects of your child's life, it's important to take into account her temperament, her level of security at home, and her readiness to interact socially. Before deciding to introduce her to the larger world outside her front door, observe how well she deals with separation from you and how attentive she is to the other children her age whom she meets now and then. If she still clings to you constantly and prefers to sit on your lap, she probably isn't ready to separate from you yet. Assuming that you are ready to let go of her, take gradual steps to encourage this separation if you can, such as having a teenager baby-sit for a couple of hours in the afternoons. If you have already enrolled her in group care and she is not adjusting at all, there is certainly no harm in removing her. (Just be sure everyone agrees that she's not just having a temporary problem with transition.) Enormous changes take place in two-year-olds' school readiness over the course of a few months. Your child may hate attending her group care center at twenty-four months, but love it by age two and a half. Taking her out of the group care situation until she's ready may circumvent a negative beginning that would stick with her for years to come.

Of course, every two-year-old will cry now and then when Mom or Dad drops her off with another adult, and all two-year-olds are highly self-absorbed. Still, there will come a time when your child's curiosity about others will override her attachment to you, making a group experience appear less threatening and more intriguing. Two is quite young for this transformation to occur, but it *does* occur this year for some children, especially those who have already experienced multiple care-givers. If you feel your child is ready for preschool—or if you truly must leave your child in group care whether or not she's ready—make sure that the class you pick suits her needs as closely as possible. A child who tends toward shyness, has trouble with novelty, or is very sensitive to noise or crowds would be happiest in a class that's small and rela-tively serene. An active and assertive child would thrive in a setting where there's plenty of time for outdoor play. No matter what type of group care you find for your child, help her begin to adjust to the idea of it before her first day. Start talking about "school" or "play group," read stories set in classrooms, take her to visit her toddler room before her first day, arrange play dates with future classmates if possible, and make plans to linger for the first few mornings until your child feels comfortable.

Once the group program has begun, don't expect your child's good-byes to be consistent at first. Not only do preschoolers respond in very different ways to separating from their parents (just watch as one of your child's fellow students forgets to kiss her mom good-bye and dives right in, while others cling and cry), but each child behaves in a variety of ways over time. Your child may cry each morning for a week and then suddenly have no problem with your leaving. Or she may respond calmly at first, but then fall apart after four weeks. Unless your child's teacher is concerned enough to discuss the issue with you, simply mon-itor your child's adjustment and take a wait-and-see attitude.

The important thing to keep in mind is that there is no single cor-rect answer to the question of when to keep a child at home and when to enroll her in preschool or group care. The fear of appearing overpro-tective haunts parents of at-home children, just as anxiety about push-ing too hard sometimes overwhelms parents of preschoolers. In the end, the choice is a personal one based on family style, finances, parents' job requirements, and the personality, interests, and needs of the child. As long as your child has plenty to do, to discuss, and to think about, it really doesn't matter whether she's interacting with half a dozen other preschoolers or just with you.

IF YOU'RE CONCERNED
Developmental Delays

This year can be a tense one for parents of a child who may be experiencing a delay in cognitive development. It is less reassuring now, if your child has still hardly spoken a word, to assert that "toddlers have their own timetables, and she's concentrating on other skills right now." Additional pressure springs from the fact that the cutoff age for early intervention programs is usually three years. Finally, with fewer pediatric checkups in this third year, your child's doctor is less likely to notice a serious slowing down of cognitive growth.

For these reasons, it is best to err on the side of caution. Though children this age vary widely in the pace at which they acquire language and other cognitive skills (such as an ability to classify types of objects or to follow a simple storyline), consult your pediatrician if your concerns of the previous year continue. Parents are still usually the best judges of whether there is truly a problem. Certainly, if your child demonstrates a marked inability to understand your own speech, to comprehend such simple concepts as up and down and full and empty, a general obliviousness or inattention to her surroundings, or even a lack of joy in her play and learning activities, a checkup now might prevent a great deal more trouble later on.

A SNACK FOR SANTA:
MAKING MENTAL CONNECTIONS

Kaisha's third birthday has just passed, and her mother, Deborah, is deep into preparations for Christmas. Once again, she has explained the meaning of the holiday to her daughter, made and wrapped presents with her, and baked dozens of cookies. Kaisha appears as delighted with the tree and the festive atmosphere this year as she was the year before, but Deborah no longer assumes that Kaisha understands what's going on just because she seems to. She finds several different ways to explain that Christmas is all about showing other people how much you love them, and that Santa gives presents to children who share, follow the rules, and are "good" boys and girls.

On Christmas Eve, Deborah, her mother, and Kaisha prepare cookies and milk for Santa to find when he comes down the chimney, and Kaisha dictates a note for Deborah to leave for him as well. The next morning, Deborah is once again ready with the video camera as her daughter is ushered into the living room to survey her gifts. This time Kaisha is as happy and excited as Deborah had hoped. She runs to inspect her new paints and easel but pauses as she passes the plate of cookies they'd left for Santa. "Look, Mama," she says, pointing to the plate. "Santa ate our cookies!" She nods to herself. "We shared."

Deborah is delighted to have the moment on videotape—but even more satisfied to see that her daughter has begun to understand ideas more completely than even a few months ago. Her words, imagination, memory, and ability to make connections between thoughts have all come together to create a whole much greater than its many parts. To a large degree, her basic brain development is now complete, and she stands on the threshold of true childhood.

ADVANCES
Common Cognitive Achievements in the Second Year

24 MONTHS May understand general time-related words such as "later" and "soon," but not more specific concepts such as "in ten minutes" or "next Monday"

27 MONTHS Able to classify objects (a cow is an animal)

More aware of conversations around her

	May understand concept of counting (one apple, two apples)
	Able to make simple mental associations
30 MONTHS	May sort objects by colors or shapes
	Can follow a storyline
33 MONTHS	Remembers much of what you tell her
	Has trouble distinguishing real from pretend
36 MONTHS	Likes to describe events that have happened or that could happen
	Engages in more elaborate imaginary play
	May be able to draw a simple face

FIRST-PERSON SINGULAR

Now record your observations of your own child's cognitive development. How does she demonstrate improvements in her memory as the months pass? When does she begin to tell you about events that happened to her recently, or to look forward to what will happen later in the day? What kinds of schemes does she come up with, and how successfully is she able to carry them out? What negotiating tools does she develop as she grows older? Does she prefer to express herself through language, drawing, physical activity, or in some other way? What kinds of stories does she like best? Does she have an imaginary friend or a favorite stuffed animal with which she likes to talk? If so, write down its name and a description. She'll enjoy reading about it when she's older.

READER'S NOTES

_____

_____

_____

_____

_____

_____

_____

_____

_____

_____

_____

_____

_____

_____

_____

_____

_____

_____

CHAPTER 4

"I Seed a Plane!"— My Verbal Abilities

N o matter what your child's level of verbal ability, the number of words he can understand dramatically exceeds the number of words he can say.

"Come on, Dylan, we've got to go pick up Daddy at his office," Linda says as she half-drags her son from the living room where our neighborhood play group has assembled. The weekly get-together has gone well, with both kids and parents eager to spend time together, but the half-dozen two-year-olds are worn out, and a number of minor crises are taking place all around the room. Dylan seems to be having an especially hard time. He's had so much fun building a block fortress with Zack that he can't imagine ever leaving this place. Nevertheless, his mother keeps pleading. "Please, Dylan," she begs as he digs his heels into the carpet. Then, lowering her voice to keep the other parents from hearing, she adds desperately, "If you come on right now, I'll stop off at McDonald's and buy you a Happy Meal."

"No way!" Dylan roars as Linda pulls on his arm. He doesn't know quite what the phrase means, but he's learned that it's quite effective in situations like this. "Gimme blocks!" Trying to make a break for it, he turns and races back toward the block fortress, but his mother catches him midstride. "Nooooooo!" Dylan roars, teetering on the edge of a tantrum. Kicking and writhing, he fights to get free of his mother. When she won't let him go, he finally sits down on the carpet, hugging his knees and clenching his fists to make himself as immovable as possible. "No go!" he announces flatly. His mother sighs and lets him go. "What am I going to do with you?" she mutters under her breath. Dylan senses her frustration, but right now he doesn't care how much he's disappointed his mom. He's effectively communicated his desire with his words and his body, and for the moment at least, he is exactly where he wants to be.

Age two is a prime time for learning new words, but for many parents a toddler's ability to "use his words" in place of kicks and crying can't come soon enough. Though your child already understands between one thousand and two thousand words and may even be able to use more than two hundred of them, sometimes in two- or three-word sentences, he still expresses himself physically much more often than through language. Limited by imperfect comprehension, intense and sometimes overwhelming emotions, and a vocabulary new enough to be easily forgotten in times of stress, your twenty-four-month-old may still hold up his arms rather than ask to be picked up. He may speak in confusingly pared-down sentences ("Mommy car!") and, like Dylan, turn himself into an immovable lump rather than discuss why he doesn't want to leave. He is as likely to repeat a word or phrase for its emotional impact as for its meaning ("Stupidhead!") as he savors all aspects of his developing verbal skills.

Fortunately, your child's communication skills will advance at a rocket pace this year—not only in the realms of vocabulary and grammar but in his ability to sustain a conversation, address adults and other children in appropriate ways, and express his desires and emotions in a socially acceptable manner. As we will see in this chapter, you and his other caregivers will act as a major force behind this growth. Your daily interactions with him will enhance his ability to converse. Your willingness to read plenty of storybooks will instill a love of language and provide structure for further learning. Your patience as he journeys from physical toward verbal expressiveness will convince him that the effort is worth the trouble. By the end of this year, your child's urgent gestures will have evolved into complex sentences, and his stubborn "No!" will have developed into somewhat more sophisticated arguments, explanations, and rationalizations. His questions will start (and won't stop), beginning with, "What dat?" and continuing with, "But why?" As he celebrates his third birthday, he will not be a perfect speaker, but he will certainly have mastered basic sentence construction and an extraordinary number of new vocabulary words—excellent tools to use in expressing himself more fully to you.

A CHILD'S-EYE VIEW
"Spoil Brat!"

Thirty-three-month-old Pete likes to go to the grocery store. The grocery cart seat seems designed just for him, and Mom often lets him pick out the treats he likes best. He is in a feisty mood today as he and Mom roll up to the checkout line, and he quickly becomes bored by the wait. He jiggles his foot restlessly, gazing around for something to entertain him.

Just then another mommy with a baby pulls her cart up behind Pete in line. *Baby!* Pete peers over his mom's shoulder at the back of the one-year-old. *Looka me!* he wills, staring at the baby, but she won't turn around and make eye contact. "Hi!" he says in a loud voice. Still no response.

Pete sighs, kicking harder against the grocery cart. Suddenly he remembers a phrase he's heard many times, most recently at the playground this morning. The words got everyone's attention. In an instant, the words are out of his mouth. "Spoil brat!" he yells at the top of his lungs, pointing at the baby.

Both his mom and the other one give Pete a shocked look—just like the mommies on the playground! Pete is thrilled, but then the other mom turns her cart so that her child's back is more fully turned to Pete. "Pete, that's not nice," his mom says loudly, very embarrassed. But Pete hardly hears her. He is determined to make contact with the baby. "Spoil brat! Poopy head!" he shrieks.

"Peter John!" The cart jerks forward, and Mom begins unloading groceries onto the conveyor belt. *Mom's mad.* Pete watches solemnly as Mom, red-faced, apologizes to the other mommy and waits for the cashier to total up her bill. Finally, Mom loads the bagged groceries into the cart, thanks the cashier, and starts pushing the cart away.

Pete perks up. He knows what to say to cashiers. "Thankoo," he coos.

"You're welcome!" The cashier waves good-bye.

Mom smiles. "That was very polite, Pete," she says, putting her head close to his as they head for the door. "I'm glad you were nice to the lady." She adds, more calmly than before, "And you should talk nicer to babies, too!"

Wow, Pete thinks as they exit the store, *some words make Mom mad. Some words make Mom smile.* He ponders this concept while she buckles him into his car seat. Then he decides, *I like it when Mom smiles.*

"GIMME MORE, PWEEZE!": VERBAL ACHIEVEMENTS IN THE FIRST THREE YEARS

"Up, Daddy." "Thankoo." "Doggie, comeer!" What can be more satisfying than hearing these early attempts at real communication from our two-year-olds? Our excitement over the prospect of getting to know our children better through their words is matched in intensity only by our children's urge to use language to relate better to their world. Both desires—ours and theirs—fuel the extraordinary leap in vocabulary and conversation throughout this year. Still, as in other areas of your child's growth, his language development began long before you heard his first words. From birth and even before, his brain began building the connections necessary to understand and use speech by taking in enormous amounts of verbal information and finding the patterns of tone, rhythm, and melody within it. This pattern-detecting process worked so efficiently, research shows, that your baby could distinguish between your language and a foreign tongue only a few days after birth. As an infant, he could tell the difference between rhymed verse and unrhymed prose. By age four months, he was sufficiently aware of the sounds of his native language to begin experimenting with sounds himself, playing with variations in pitch and loudness. Soon he could manage strings of consonant-vowel syllables ("ba-ba-ba-ba-ba"). As more patterns were perceived and more neuronal connections made in his brain, he improved his ability to mimic the sounds you made, until he was babbling with such adult-like rhythms and tones that it was easy to forget he wasn't actually talking. (It's interesting to note that deaf babies, who aren't able to benefit from this listening and analyzing process, start out making sounds like hearing children, but then begin to falter when they reach the "ba-ba-ba" stage at six months.)

Your child's brain continued to mark how often he heard particular sounds as he attempted his first words. These words were among those he most frequently heard—or at least noticed the most because they were uttered by those he loved. By around eighteen months (though the "normal" age ranges from thirteen to twenty-five months), his listening, processing, and practicing of speech reached a critical mass, and your child began comprehending (though not necessarily speaking) as many as five or six new words a day. Most were nouns, along with some pronouns ("me," "mine"), common phrases ("That's enough!"), and a verb now and then.

Now, at the beginning of his third year, your child may well have begun using two-word sentences, such as "No nap" or "Bottle juice," and attempting longer strings of words that have caught his fancy even if he doesn't know what they mean ("You are my sunshine, my only sunshine . . ."). The rate of verbal development among two-year-olds continues to vary widely, but no matter what their level of ability, their *receptive vocabulary*—the words they can understand even if they don't use them—will continue to dramatically exceed their *productive vocabulary*—the number of words they can say.

Once your child can paste two words together, it won't be long before he starts creating true sentences. Meanwhile, his vocabulary will expand exponentially as he casually picks up a word you say over breakfast and makes it his before the end of the day. The more words he commands, the more important it becomes to organize them in some way—and grammar comes to his rescue in the nick of time. By age two and a half, he will probably have begun adding "-s" to create plural forms for his nouns; soon he'll add an "-ing" to a verb or two (even when it's incorrect), and then "-ed" for the past tense. As we will see later in this chapter, researchers are still unsure how much of this sudden burst of grammatical ability is innate and how much comes from his brain's attention to the patterns of the language he hears. In any case, the result is that your child's sentences will be much more complex in structure, and clearer in content, by the end of this year. As a three-year-old, he will use words to express his ideas and feelings almost as naturally as an adult.

A PARENT'S STORY
"I'm Not Resty"

"When Nina was one, everybody used to tell me she was an incredibly verbal child," another mother told me as she watched her three-year-old play with the toys in our pediatrician's waiting room. "She only had to hear something said once, and before the hour was up she'd have repeated it two or three times. Not just single words, but whole strings of them, like 'Twinkle, Twinkle, Little Star,' or her street address.

"Then, all of a sudden, when she was about two and a half, it was like her whole ability to speak kind of disintegrated. She started saying 'eated' instead of 'ate,' 'runned' instead of 'ran.'

Sometimes she talked so fast that her pronunciation went downhill, too. Lots of times we just couldn't figure out what she was saying. I started to wonder if she was having developmental problems. But then a friend of mine told me she'd read that toddlers' grammar falls apart because they're no longer imitating our speech but actually creating it on their own. Of course, kids would make mistakes in that case, with all our irregular verbs and complicated sentences!

"It was a relief to know that Nina's speech was normal for her age, but I didn't start to really appreciate the process until right around her third birthday. We'd had a long day, and I was slumped on the living room sofa watching her wander around. She started crying over nothing, and I said, 'I guess it's about rest time, huh?'

" 'I'm not resty,' she answered, snuggling against me.

" 'Well, I think you are a little tired,' I said, putting an arm around her.

" 'No, I amn't!' she said.

"I had to laugh. Talking with her was so hit-or-miss sometimes. But it was nothing like the 'Twinkle Twinkles' from a year ago. Back then, she probably didn't understand half of what she was saying—she just liked the sounds of the words or the reactions she got. This, on the other hand, was a real conversation. She communicated her feelings and understood my answers. She knows that words mean something now, and she can use them to get what she wants and build relationships with the people in her life.

"I still correct her grammar all the time, of course. But she's gotten better at expressing herself, and I've figured out that with talking it's the content, not the package, that really counts."

"THANKOO!": GUESSING AT MEANINGS AND LEARNING THE RULES

"Okay, Sarah," the dad said wearily to his wailing two-year-old, glancing at the impatient line behind them at the ice cream store. "I *see* that you don't want vanilla this time. How about chocolate? Just tell me what you want instead of yelling—please?"

His daughter's continued fussing must have made this dad regret having offered her an ice cream in the first place. But they had probably been having such fun shopping together—and his little girl had seemed so grown-up and well behaved—that he forgot how limited her resources still were. He was surprised when Sarah reacted to the ice cream crisis with a tantrum, yet her collapse under the pressure of her still-limited cognition and difficulty with language and the overwhelming frustration that resulted were perfectly normal for her age. She had only truly figured out the concept that words can be used to name objects about six to eight months before—and now she was faced with using them to express her feelings and get the flavor she wanted. Hard as it is for parents to keep in mind, making the journey from physical toward verbal communication is just as hard for the two-year-old as it is for those who love him—particularly when he's tired, hungry, or otherwise stressed.

If you have ever tried to learn a foreign language, you know that learning to speak is not just about memorizing words, obeying grammatical rules, and refining one's pronunciation. It also involves such social skills as taking turns in conversation, recognizing and repairing misunderstandings, and using language in polite, culturally appropriate ways. Two-year-olds must learn all these rules of communication, too—but without the experience or resources we have. To get her ice cream, Sarah must know not only how to say the words, "I don't want vanilla. I want chocolate," but how to get her father's attention, express her desire (preferably with a "please"), listen to his response, and clarify any confusion—all while controlling her strong fear that she will not end up with what she wants. This social dimension of language—its ability to enhance communication between two people—is not an instinctive process. It must be learned.

You have been helping your child learn the social skills of language practically from the day he was born. By responding to his facial expressions, gestures, and early vocalizations—and by playing such games as peekaboo—you introduced your baby to the idea of taking turns. By his first birthday, he was no doubt entranced by the rhythmic give-and-take of human conversation and had begun working hard to respond to your words with appropriate sounds, expressions, and movement. Another skill you taught your child by example was that of *joint attention*—the tendency to share a focus of conversation. When chatting with your preverbal baby, you often tried to direct his attention to particular objects or talked about things that already had his attention. As a result, he learned to use the direction of your gaze to determine which object you were labeling. This not only familiarized him with the name of the object but introduced him to the concept that the two of you were *communicating* about the object, not just making random noises. Soon he began trying to communicate back, using sounds and gestures to try to "tell" you something. If you failed to understand what he was trying to express, he probably got frustrated, but he also tried to fix the problem by repeating or changing his sounds, gestures, and behavior.

As much as the process of communicating with you thrilled your baby, he still did not really understand the fact that the words you were saying were *names* for things. When you cried, "Doggie," when a dog came up and licked your face, he didn't know whether "doggie" referred to the dog, to what it was doing, or to your feelings about it. As a result, he usually spoke his own first word ("Mama," "doggie," "cookie") because he found himself in the same situation in which he'd heard it, not because he clearly understood its meaning. Only after many more months of exposure to these words was he able to remember them, link the situations in which he'd heard them to create a category of objects that they represented, and then actually produce them. By around eighteen months, however, he began to understand that "doggie" *meant* "dog"—not only his own dog but all the other dogs in picture books, on the street, and in conversation. Once this amazing realization dawned on him, he probably dropped many of his first, improperly understood vocabulary words and threw himself into a frenzied acquisition of nouns, names, and familiar phrases, incessantly asking, "What that?"

The more words he learned, the more eagerly your toddler tried to use them to communicate his desires, feelings, and intentions to you. He crammed as much meaning as he could into his limited vocabulary. "Doggie!" could mean, "I'm scared of the dog," "Where is the dog?" "Look at that dog," and so on. As a result, you were often confused by his utterances. You frequently had to guess what he was trying to tell you in a game of fill-in-the-blank. Though he usually tried to clarify his message, he wasn't always successful. Many a one-year-old's tantrum has sprung from just such a breakdown in communication.

Now, at around his second birthday, the situation has begun to ease somewhat. A growing understanding of verbs and adjectives allows your child to create clearer, if still very short, sentences. Accustomed to figuring out the meanings of words by pointing to the object you're talking about or saying the same word each time an object appears, he can now quickly guess the meaning of a word from its context. This guessing process, called *fast mapping,* was illustrated in a 1987 study by Tracy Heibeck and Ellen Markman of the University of Pittsburgh. Experimenters exposed two- to four-year-olds to unfamiliar terms for colors, shapes, and textures. In each case, the experimenter placed the unfamiliar word in the context of familiar ones, as in, "Bring me the chartreuse one. Not the blue one, the chartreuse one." When the children were tested a few minutes later, even the two-year-olds showed that they had correctly learned the new words.

Your child's fast mapping skills will take off this year, greatly enhancing his ability to expand his vocabulary. Research using magnetic resonance imaging (MRI) has shown that a typical fifteen-month-old needs more than a second to recognize even a familiar word, like "bottle," while an eighteen-month-old guesses the word slightly before the speaker has finished saying it. By age twenty-four months, however, the child guesses the word in only six hundred milliseconds—the moment the first syllable ("bot-") is spoken. This increased speed enables him to process much more information as he listens.

Your two-year-old's desire to communicate his thoughts to you will remain passionate and intense throughout this period. Like Sarah, he will continue to feel overwhelmed emotionally at times when he realizes he's misunderstood, and he will keep experimenting with new words, tones of voice, and behaviors in his efforts to make you understand. You can help him learn new ways to communicate effectively by frequently demonstrating useful verbal formulas or routines ("Hi," "How are you?" "Bye-bye," "Please," "Thank you," "Excuse me") and tactfully raising his consciousness of the volume of his speech ("It's time to use your indoor voice") and his tone ("I can't understand you when you whine").

As he approaches his third birthday, he will appreciate your efforts to supply him with longer verbal *scripts* to supplement his still-limited ability to carry on a conversation on his own. A script, or conversational blueprint for certain situations, can provide your child with a general idea of appropriate behavior, along with a few key phrases that should see him through. By talking to him about what people say during certain encounters, rehearsing a new situation before it happens, and even prompting him gently during his first attempt or two, you can help your child ultimately hold his own while talking to grown-ups, ordering lunch at a restaurant, and so on. This is especially helpful as your child starts to interact more with children his age, who aren't yet willing or able to help him through the conversation the way most adults do.

As the months pass, your child's increasing mastery of the verbal routines and scripts you have taught him, as well as his improving ability to stifle his frustration and try again, will lead to more interesting and rewarding conversations over breakfast, on the way to the sitter's, at rest time, and during all the other little moments the two of you share each day. He will still be motivated to communicate more from a desire to get what he wants than a willingness to listen to what you have to say. (He will become much more upset if he can't make you understand that he wants the train in the toy store window than if he doesn't understand what you're telling him about his missing boot.) As the year progresses, however, he'll become more interested in your viewpoint and those of others. How quickly this happens will depend on his particular temperament, the pace of his emotional and social development, and his vocabulary skills, but by the end of this year all the tools for effective communication should be in place. The day will soon come when you realize with a start that the two of you have really started to "talk."

Playing with Words

A great number of studies have demonstrated that the more parents talk with their children when they are toddlers, the larger the children's vocabularies will be by the time they start school. "Just chatting"—pointing out, naming, and discussing objects in the environment—is certainly an effective way to teach your child new words, but specific techniques can enhance your child's verbal growth even more.

Rhyming is a form of wordplay that all toddlers love—as you know from your experiences with nursery rhymes, children's songs, and every book by Dr. Seuss. Rhyming also stimulates your child's ear for language because it encourages him to pay attention to the specific sounds in every word. While you are helping your child dress in the morning or waiting in line at the gas station, invent funny rhymes about what the two of you are doing and encourage him to finish them. You can stimulate his thinking about the meanings of words and the rhythms of language by making up stories with him (even very short ones), making puns and word jokes ("Gooseberry? It doesn't look like a goose to me"), and talking about the different meanings of a single word. Try to include plenty of generalizations ("All taxis are yellow"), categories ("A parrot is a kind of bird"), and comparisons ("That horse hopped like a rab-

Stay close and narrate events as your two-year-old navigates his way through an exciting new world of words and symbols.

bit!") in your conversations. As he grows increasingly able to follow a storyline, show him how stories relate to experience by telling him tales about children his age, reading him picture books that relate to his current interests, and recalling brief stories about your childhood ("When I was two . . .").

Just be sure you're not talking *at* your child, but talking *with* him. Pause long enough for him to process your words. Wait for his responses. By really listening to what *he* has to say, you can create a pattern of rich communication that will last for years to come.

"HE RUNNED AND RUNNED!": EXPERIMENTING WITH GRAMMAR

As hard as parents work at increasing their children's understanding of how the world operates, how people interact, and how to deal with a variety of emotions, it's a relief to know that we don't have to sit our two-year-olds down and give them lessons in grammar, too. Children in the middle of their third year experience a breathtaking growth spurt in grammatical development all on their own as they move from the typical twenty-four-month-old's "Me Tarzan" type of speech toward more complex sentences that include verbs, articles, pronouns, prepositions, prefixes, and suffixes ("My name's Tarzan. What's yours?"). By his third birthday, your child will have acquired not only a vocabulary of several thousand words but, as the MIT scientist Steven Pinker writes in his book *The Language Instinct*, "a tacit knowledge of grammar more sophisticated than the thickest style manual." Best of all, he will have taken this leap with little conscious effort on your own part. Research shows that parents pay much more attention to the content of their young children's statements than to their grammar—yet most children learn correct grammar anyway.

Not only will your child develop his grammar skills this year, but he will develop them in the same order (if not necessarily the same rate) as other children his age. First, he will begin adding "-s" to his nouns and "-ing" to his verbs when appropriate. Somewhat later, you will hear a past-tense suffix ("-ed") and the "-s" suffix to form the third-person singular ("He laughs and laughs"). Once these conventions have been mastered, he will begin using contractions ("It's my turn," or, "They're funny"), and somewhere along the way he will have picked up such useful "function" words as "some," "would," "how," and "after." Of course, your child's grammar will not always be correct (there are plenty of irregular words, such as "ran" and "mice," to trip him up), but it will always be logical. Over time, his errors will diminish as he compares his own grammar with what he hears from others.

For decades, this sequence of grammatical skills was considered as instinctive for children as song for a bird. MIT linguist Noam Chomsky pointed out more than thirty years ago that virtually every language in the world is created from noun phrases ("Joey's mommy") and verb phrases ("drove the car"). Noting that two-year-olds seem to instinctively understand this structure and to use it themselves as they begin to create their own sentences, Chomsky suggested that there must be a universal grammar hardwired into the brain and shared by all human beings. Research over the past decade, however, has challenged this idea. MRI studies show that young children's brains respond to patterns in their parents' grammar in much the same way as they notice frequencies in sound and vocabulary words. Computer programs designed to simulate the working brain, called "neural nets," automatically sort words into categories—just as a child learns that certain kinds of words refer to actions while others refer to objects—and figure out some rules of word order. Neural nets even make many of the same mistakes that children do ("He jumped me the ball"). Clearly, though operating on a much more primitive level than that of a human brain, such neural nets have taken in enormous amounts of verbal information and found the regular patterns within it. Perhaps that is what your child is doing, too.

The debate between the relative contributions of nature (your child's instinctive grammatical ability) and nurture (how much he has learned by example) continues. No doubt, as with other aspects of his development, both are constantly at work as he grows. He may naturally tend to look for the grammatical elements of your speech, in other words, but you must provide plenty of that speech (and a wide variety of it) if he is to put his tendencies to practical use. At this age, you needn't strictly monitor his sentence construction, of course. (The day will come when you miss his charming mistakes.) Just provide him with examples in your everyday conversation, in storybooks, and through the media, correct him on his own efforts gently now and then, and praise him for the progress he makes.

As natural as his progression from "Up, Mommy!" to "Pick me up, Mommy!" may seem this year, it's hard not to appreciate the dramatic accomplishments of your two-year-old. Not only has he internalized and learned to reproduce the rhythms, tones, and sound combinations of his native language, but he has grown to understand their meanings in a wide variety of contexts and has learned many of the social situations in which they can be used. Not only has he picked up on what order the words must be in to make sense, but he's figured out which supporting words are necessary to flesh out his sentence and even, in most cases, which words do not follow the general grammatical rules. (If he lives in a bilingual home, he has probably learned to do this in two languages!) By the time he is three, 90 percent of his sentences will be grammatically correct. Not a bad record after only three years.

IF YOU'RE CONCERNED
Verbal Delays

Waiting for a child to move from single words to sentences can be a painful process for the parents of two-year-olds—especially since adults so frequently (and often erroneously) equate verbal ability with general intelligence. The questions and comments of friends and relatives ("What's he saying? I can't understand him.") certainly don't ease the pressure. In fact, children this age continue to vary widely in their verbal abilities, and your child's reluctance to speak may just be a manifestation of his particular temperament or unique circumstances. When considering whether his development is within the "normal" range, keep in mind that few two-year-olds (or even three-year-olds) are fully comprehensible. Most lisp, slur their words, mispronounce such letters as "l," "v," and "r," and stutter as they try to make their mouths keep up with their thoughts. Also remember that twins tend to speak later than single children—as do premature children—and their speech development may continue to lag behind a bit for much of this year. Major events at home, such as the birth of a sibling or a change in child-care arrangements, may also create a temporary pause or regression in his speech. Even under normal circumstances, two-year-olds may briefly lose their speech skills rather easily, especially near the beginning of this year. Your child's speech will probably diminish when he's deeply engaged in play, and he may well fall silent when a new person enters the room and greets him. In both cases, he simply doesn't yet have the cognitive energy to deal with the experience and create speech at the same time.

Yet there are, of course, instances when a child's relative silence may indicate a problem with speech. The first indicator is your own gut feeling about how he is progressing. Does he seem seriously out of place or uncomfortable when playing with his more verbal peers? Does he communicate with others easily through gestures and simple words, and understand what they are saying to him? What do the parents of his friends think about his speech? How long have you been worried about his progress? Often your own sense that something is wrong is the best "first warning" that will lead to help for your child. Other red flags regarding verbal development include an inability to understand differences in meaning (up versus down), to follow two requests ("Please pick up the bottle and give it to me"), to maintain eye contact during conversation, to string together two or three words, or to name common objects.

If you suspect that your child is having too much trouble with any of these aspects of verbal development, it is important to discuss your concerns with his pediatrician or a speech pathologist *as soon as possible*. If the cause is hearing loss or a neurological disorder, the earlier your child's delay is diagnosed and treated, the better the chance that his brain can reorganize, and the more easily he may be able to catch up. Even profoundly deaf children should be exposed to sign language as early as possible to take advantage of the two-year-old's critical period of language development. In the realm of speech, a parent's philosophy should be "Let's look into it now," not, "Let's wait and see."

"HE DOESN'T TALK MUCH": THE LINK BETWEEN VERBAL ABILITY AND INTELLIGENCE

"I love my little boy, but he worries me sometimes," a friend told me over lunch. "Mack started preschool this year, and every day when I pick him up he's off in the corner by himself, playing with a truck or a pile of blocks. Some of the other kids are talking up a storm, and even though I know he *can* talk when he really wants to, I almost never see him do it. My daughter was talking in whole paragraphs by this time. Frankly, I'm starting to wonder if he just isn't as smart as she is."

Such concerns are common but, as I pointed out earlier, very frequently unfounded. We have seen in this chapter that a large part of language development involves listening. The brain of a quiet child is likely to be quite busily processing not only vocabulary and grammatical rules but any of the many other concepts he must master this year. As several experts have pointed out, proof that the areas of language and cognition are quite different is found in a rare genetic disorder called Williams syndrome. Children with this disability can speak in full, complex sentences, tell a beautiful story, and employ such communication skills as looking a person in the eye as they speak, asking questions, and so on. Nevertheless, their IQ scores generally hover in the seventies—substantially below average.

Still, cognition and language are clearly linked in some ways, and one activity supports and enhances the other in your child's brain. A certain level of cognition, or comprehension, is necessary for your child to begin expressing himself through words. The development of memory and symbolic thinking (such as the ability to picture an object or action) is also necessary before a child can move forward with language. Your child's surge in vocabulary that began at about eighteen months was strongly connected to his ability to sort objects into categories. Scientists have long linked two-year-olds' block-building, memory, and symbolic play to their efforts to combine two or more words. In turn, learning new words stimulates aspects of a child's intelligence, such as curiosity. Over the past few decades, through magnetic resonance imaging, researchers have been able to watch as a new word literally forms new connections in a child's brain.

Your child's cognitive potential and rate of language development are no doubt partly inherited. Still, when so much improvement is possible in each area by making use of the other, it makes sense during this year to keep the links between them in mind. Allow your child plenty of time to play with blocks, dolls, and other kids, and don't forget to talk with him about his play. These moments spent placing one wooden cube atop another, whispering secrets to his puppet, interacting with children his age, and describing his exploits to you are the solid pedestal on which much of his future comprehension and expression will be built.

THE TOY BOX
At Twenty-eight Months

Nat is playing with his action figures on the floor of the living room while his older brother, Andrew, plays checkers nearby with a friend. "Jumped you," Andrew says, moving his piece over one of his friend's. Nat looks up, intrigued. *Jumped?* he thinks. He didn't see Andrew jump!

Nat gets up, goes over to the table where the boys are playing, and watches as Andrew's friend makes a move. "Jumped you!" Nat crows triumphantly.

The boys laugh. "No, Nat, he didn't jump me," Andrew tells him. "This is jumping. If my piece is here, see, and his piece is there . . ." Andrew demonstrates "jumping" in checkers for Nat. "Get it?" he asks.

Nat nods importantly. He likes it when Andrew pays attention to him. As the boys continue playing, he goes back to his action figures. "Take that!" he murmurs, smashing the two figures against each other. Then he gets an idea. Pressing one figure to the floor, he makes the other leap over it, much as Andrew's checkers piece sailed over that of his friend. "Jumped you!" he says excitedly. As the older boys continue their own game, Nat "jumps" his action figures again and again.

"READ ME A STORY": DEVELOPING A LOVE OF LANGUAGE

"Wead me a story, pweeeze?" What parent hasn't heard this plea from his two-year-old—often when he was just about to settle down to the TV or the newspaper or start a conversation with his spouse. Beginning at age two or even earlier, nearly all young children become entranced by the power of a simple story accompanied by bright, comprehensible pictures. If your child has his way, you will find yourself reading much more than the occasional bedtime story this year.

If so, it will be a wonderful boon to your child as he develops his language skills, since even at this young age storytime can enhance later performance in school. Research indicates that children who are read to frequently at home learn to read relatively easily once they start school. The kind of dialogue parents typically engage in while reading ("What's that? A kitty! Right! And what's that? Yes, a hen!") resembles the kind used in school and thus paves the way for school success.

Fortunately, storytime—one of the few times when many active two-year-olds are willing to settle into a parent's lap and have a conversation—can be at least as pleasant for parents as it is for kids. As a result, it's one parental duty with which it's pretty easy to comply—once we set aside our beliefs about how a child should behave while we read to him. At age two, in fact, listening to a story should be an active pursuit. Ask your child to name objects in the illustrations, to fill in the blanks (especially with rhymed verse, which offers your child a clue), and to comment on the plot, the characters, and anything he's

Be ready to support your two-year-old as storybooks and a budding imagination fill her head with all sorts of emotions.

reminded of by the story. As his language skills improve, ask more complex questions about the text ("How does Red Riding Hood know that that's the wolf in her granny's nightgown?"), and introduce new books with more complex texts and pictures. Be sure to talk about the stories you've read at other times during the day ("Wow, this must be how Babar felt when the elephants made him king"). In this way, you'll teach him that books are related to life in intimate ways. Keep in mind, though, that at this age it's more important to have fun reading together than for your child to answer your questions correctly or for you to finish the story. Choosing books with characters who are already familiar to him, and series of books that you can think about together adds to his pleasure, giving him a sense of familiarity and continuity.

Q & A
"Fee, Fi, Fo, Fum!"

Q: When my daughter was born, her uncle gave her a beautiful, leather-bound book of fairy tales. The illustrations are gorgeous, and I love the book myself, so I've been reading the stories to my daughter since she was a baby. But now that she's starting to understand more of the words, and her imagination is taking off, I wonder whether they're really appropriate for her. After all, Jack climbs up a beanstalk, steals a hideous giant's personal belongings, and then kills him rather than give them back! And what about Hansel and Gretel, left to die in the woods by their parents and nearly eaten by a witch? Are fairy tales okay for children this age?

A: It can be startling, as you first begin to read to your child, to realize just how violent and frightening many traditional stories are. One reason for this is that most of them were first told or written long before children were considered children—that is, before they were understood to be different in important ways from adults. Deciding whether they are too frightening for your child is largely a personal matter, but it's unlikely that the stories will actually harm your child in any lasting way. In fact, the renowned psychoanalyst Bruno Bettelheim passionately insisted that children need fairy tales. He believed that the stories' brutality touches children's own unexpressed fears and helps them work out ways of mastering them. He was also convinced that the unreality of fairy tales offers children a safety zone in which to explore their feelings of vulnerability.

Still, be aware of the combined effect of words and pictures. (Pictures sometimes frighten two-year-olds more than words.) Since your child can't read yet, you're free to skip over some of the scarier parts. Keep in mind that more recently written books usually take children's developmental level into account and can also stimulate and entertain them when combined with more traditional tales.

"USE YOUR WORDS": MOVING FROM PHYSICAL TO VERBAL EXPRESSION

A year has passed, but the parents-and-toddlers group in our neighborhood still meets once a week. A few younger kids have joined up over the past months, and several older children have dropped out as they entered preschool, but Dylan and his mom, Linda, are still active members. Dylan continues to hate leaving at the end of a session, and his mother has decided he's a kid who doesn't like transitions. Fortunately, she's learned to plan ahead by preparing afternoon activities and other inducements to lure him home. Dylan has gradually improved in his ability to negotiate with her, too.

Today, Linda tells me, she's just grateful Dylan no longer yells "Jerk!" at her when she says it's time to leave, as he did for most of his thirty-third month. (While unsettling, this type of inappropriate language usage is very typical of the progression toward productive conversation.) In fact, Dylan's progress from sit-down strikes at twenty-four months to more reasonable requests at age three to "stay longer" has been full of detours and regressions. During a long month when his father was out of town on business, for example, Dylan reverted to shrieks and name-calling before he found his nice words again. And there are bad days even now, particularly when Dylan is tired or overstimulated.

Fortunately, Linda has felt supported by the other moms' understanding this year, and our assurances that all our kids are facing similar challenges. She's worked hard at talking with Dylan about his experience when leaving a place, and she has read stories to him that seemed to relate to his fears about change. By now it is clear that Dylan knows his own heart better than he did a year ago and is more able to express exactly why he doesn't want to go away. "Stay five more minutes, Mom?" I overhear him asking his mom.

"No, Dylan. You know we talked about that," she responds.

"I want to play with Nathan," he announces, trying another ploy.

"Nathan's leaving now, too. Let's go home and play that new game we bought yesterday, okay? I get the green marker this time!"

Dylan considers. "I like the green one," he points out.

"Well, that's true. Green's your favorite color, isn't it? Okay, you can have the green marker if you come with me right now."

Dylan glances over his shoulder. He sees that the play group is breaking up. "Okay," he says. "But I want an ice cream cone, too."

"We'll talk about it over lunch." Linda shoots an exasperated look over her shoulder at us. We can sympathize. As all parents know, verbal interaction with a thirty-six-month-old can sometimes be almost as difficult as the nonverbal kind. Older two-year-olds love to discuss, negotiate, and demand endless explanations and concessions. In the long run, however, these first attempts at communication are well worth the effort. With your encouragement, your young child will learn to express his ideas clearly, find new ways to understand and manage his emotions, and experience the wonderful sense that others care very much about what he has to say.

ADVANCES
Common Verbal Achievements in the Third Year

24 MONTHS	Can probably make two-, three-, or four-word sentences
	Mimics adult inflections and phrases
	Starts using pronouns (usually "I" and "me")
27 MONTHS	Speaks clearly most of the time
	Vocabulary grows rapidly

30 MONTHS	Can name some body parts
	May name some colors
33 MONTHS	Uses prepositions ("on," "in," "over")
	Carries on two- to three-sentence conversations
	Can name some objects in a book
36 MONTHS	Can follow a two- or three-part command
	Speaks in four- to five-word sentences
	Diction may still be imperfect

FIRST PERSON SINGULAR

Your child's early conversation is sure to be a study in twisted logic, and in the years to come you will no doubt enjoy reviewing this record of his first attempts to convince you of something or tell you a story. Nevertheless, two-year-olds also come up with amazingly perceptive comments now and then, and these are certainly worth recording as well. If possible, make an audio- or videotape of your child speaking this year so that you can compare it to how he expresses himself in the years to come. You will be amazed at how completely his tone, gestures, pronunciation, and vocabulary are transformed over the next months. Capture his first expressions now before they're gone forever.

READER'S NOTES

_____

_____

_____

_____

_____

_____

_____

_____

_____

_____

_____

_____

_____

_____

_____

_____

_____

_____

_____

_____

_____

_____

_____

_____

_____

_____

_____

_____

_____

_____

_____

_____

_____

_____

_____

_____

_____

_____

_____

_____

_____

_____

_____

CHAPTER 5

Pride and Anxiety— My Emotional Growth

At some point around the middle of this year, your child will make her first connections between how she feels at one moment and how she feels the next.

Marjorie isn't just having a bad day—she's having a terrible one. First thing this morning, she got a call from her soon-to-be ex-husband, Nick, demanding more visitation with their daughter, Megan. The argument that ensued made Marjorie late to work, where rumors were flying that the company was planning another round of layoffs. Marjorie has been working there for only a few months, since just after Megan's second birthday. She's pretty certain she'll be one of the first to go.

Today Marjorie has a late meeting, which makes her half an hour late picking up Megan at the sitter's. She drives as fast as she can across town, trying to fight off the guilt she always feels when she thinks about how much time Megan spends away from her now. If Marjorie and her husband had stayed together, Marjorie probably would have stayed home full-time until Megan was three or four. She still hasn't adjusted to the idea of putting her daughter in someone else's care.

Marjorie arrives to find Megan and her sitter, Catherine, baking chocolate chip cookies. The kitchen smells scrumptious, and Marjorie feels her entire body relax. "Hello, sweetie," she says, giving her daughter a hug. "Ready to go?"

Instead of returning the hug, Megan turns to her mother with a terrible scowl. "Go way!" she shouts. She turns back to the cookies as her mother, hurt but hardly surprised, wonders how to respond. Megan refuses to go home almost every evening when her mother arrives to pick her up. It's as though she's transferred her loyalty to Catherine— and it feels at times as though she almost *hates* her mom.

"Hey, now, it's okay," Catherine coos, putting down her spatula and giving Megan a little pat. "She's tired," she explains to Marjorie with an apologetic smile. To Megan she adds, "Don't you want to take some cookies home for Mommy?"

"No!" Megan shrieks, slamming a handful of cookie dough on the counter. "I stay here! Don't want you!"

Marjorie can feel her anxiety return full force. First, she tries to negotiate with her daughter—offering to play a board game or string some necklaces with her when they get home. In the end, however, she has to carry Megan out to the car kicking and screaming, while Catherine smiles uncomfortably and murmurs, "I'm sure it's just a phase."

Even in the best of circumstances, life with a two-year-old can be stormy and unpredictable. Thrilled (but also sometimes overwhelmed) by the previous year's realization that she is a separate individual with thoughts, feelings, and different goals from yours, your two-year-old is committed to fortifying her new, fragile sense of self. Her need to feel powerful and autonomous, to assert some control over her environment and herself, clashes with her equally intense need for your love, approval, and support. These opposing needs rule her life for most of the year, creating emotions so heightened and constantly changing that the adults in her life can hardly keep up. When events so often take place without her approval (whether the major changes of divorce that Megan faced or the everyday surprises of altered plans and challenging new situations), it's no wonder your child swings from baby-like clinginess to loud defiance over a span of mere moments or even for weeks at a time.

Other factors help make this period emotionally challenging for the entire family. A two-year-old's preoccupation with speech development, toilet training, or other learning processes may keep her awake nights, making her more emotional during the day. Her increasing awareness of the feelings of those around her may lead her toward frightening conclusions (*Mom's mad. Maybe she doesn't love me*). Her limited ability to express her feelings in words is likely to frustrate her immensely—just as her developmental need to experiment with such negative emotions as anger and defiance will probably frustrate *you*. As a result, as Alicia Lieberman, author of *The Emotional Life of the Toddler,* points out, mild to moderate conflicts tend to take place between parent and child about every *three minutes* in homes with young children, and major conflicts happen about three times every hour. No wonder parenting a child this age feels like riding a roller coaster.

Fortunately, the same need for independence that drives your two-year-old's rebellious impulses creates some very rewarding results as well. Her growing sense of self lays the groundwork for her increasingly unique style of emotional expression, openness to novelty, and interaction with others—in short, her personality. As the months pass and she begins to explore her own imaginative, moral, and social potential, she will start to emerge from the more generic and universal behavior patterns of early toddlerhood like a butterfly from its cocoon. By the end of the year, having explored an array of new feelings (including pride, guilt, rage, tenderness, and perhaps even true empathy), she will begin to settle into a more characteristic range that reflects her *experience* as well as her temperament. The turmoil of the early months will subside as the two of you learn how to work together on expressing feelings through words rather than actions and how to find acceptable outlets for her emotions. With this goal partly achieved by the end of the year, she will have more emotional energy to interact socially with others her age and figure out how to achieve her goals in acceptable ways.

It isn't easy to give a two-year-old enough room to express her emotions while maintaining acceptable limits. Nevertheless, the rewards—in terms of her increased self-confidence, self-control, and desire to live up to your standards—are absolutely worth the effort. As you experiment with talking through conflicts, negotiating with each other, backing off at times when she's unable to talk with you, holding her when she's out of control, and using compromise, distraction, humor, and careful preparation to avoid as many rocky moments as possible, you will learn a great deal more about what works for your child and what doesn't. At the same time, you will be teaching her through example how to manage *her own* constantly fluctuating surges of desire, resentment, anger, and love. By the end of this year's journey, the two of you will have gotten to know each other—and yourselves—much better than before. You'll have a better understanding of when she needs you to guide, support, or limit her behavior and when it's okay to "give her the reins." This deeper understanding will help you both weather the many storms (and savor the triumphs) to come.

A CHILD'S-EYE VIEW
"I Won't!"

It's early morning, and Eliot's mom, Helen, is hastily getting him ready to go to Grandma's for the day. "Come on," she murmurs, shoving his legs into his sweatpants, "hurry it up, pumpkin. We're late."

Too rough, Eliot thinks grumpily, bending his legs to make the process as difficult as possible. *Want cereal!* Eliot's entire morning routine—breakfast in his pajamas at the kitchen table, time with his toys while Mommy gets dressed, and a hug from Dad before they leave—is ruined because of the early hour. *My body!* he thinks as Mommy shoves a sweater over his head. *My sweater! Mine, mine, mine!*

"Time to brush your teeth," Helen says, hauling him to his feet. Her voice sounds mad, but he's too out of sorts to care. *I can walk!* he protests silently as she lugs him to the bathroom and sets him on his stool. "Open your mouth," she commands, grabbing the toothpaste and toothbrush. "Hurry up. We're late."

"No!" Eliot clamps his jaw shut. He hates the way the toothbrush bumps against his gums. He examines his reflection in the mirror. He is intrigued by the defiant, willful face that looks back at him. His mother's obvious exasperation is satisfying, too.

"Eliot! I'm sick of this," his mother snaps. "I'm counting to three. One! Two!"

"Aaaaaaaaaaargh!" Eliot wails.

Just then, Dad's face appears in the mirror. "What? You won't brush your teeth?" he says, making a silly face at his son. Helen scowls impatiently at her husband, but steps back to give him room.

"You wanna brush your nose, then?" Dad squats down to Eliot's level.

"No," Eliot says, struggling to hold on to his anger.

"Or maybe your eyelashes," Dad says. "We have to brush Eliot's eyelashes!"

Eliot feels a giggle escape in spite of himself. "Silly!" he says with delight.

"Oh, that's not how you do it?" Dad says, giving Eliot a quick hug. "Then give me the toothbrush, Mommy. Eliot's going to show us how you *really* brush your teeth!"

With a shrug of surrender, Helen hands the toothbrush over. Proudly Eliot sticks it in his mouth and moves it around. Dad helps out a little. "So that's how it works!" Dad says. "That was great! Rinse out now, kid. We can go play while Mommy gets dressed."

Yay! Eliot hurries to rinse out his mouth. He glances at his reflection and sees a different, happier face than the one from a moment ago. He pauses. *Why was I mad?* He can't remember. But it doesn't matter. Now Eliot's the one in a hurry.

"WHERE'S MOMMY?": EMOTIONAL GROWTH IN THE FIRST TWO YEARS

"Mommy, I need a Band-Aid." The two-year-old sidles up to her mother at the playground, tears running down her face.

"Oh, honey." Her mother fumbles in her backpack for a Band-Aid and squats down to look at her daughter's knee. "Did you fall down?"

"Allie pushed me." The girl's face is a study in contrasts, the sadness over her scraped knee fighting with the satisfaction of having an interesting story to tell. "I . . . I was . . . I was on the big ladder," she explains. "I fell down."

"Well, here's a Band-Aid." Mom wipes off the scrape and ceremoniously presses the colored strip to her daughter's knee. "I'm sorry you got hurt. But you're okay now, aren't you?"

"I'm okay." The girl leans in close for a hug, her chin quivering in abject self-pity even as her mouth turns up with the pleasure of getting Mom's undivided attention. Is she sad or happy, a victim or a mother's treasured child? She hovers between opposing emotional states and self-images, not sure which to choose.

What a mixed-up, puzzling, yet fascinating experience it must be, getting through each day as a two-year-old. Veteran of an entire year's worth of independent exploration, fully aware of her status as a separate person, your child is now bombarded with a host of subtle new feelings and sensations that often do battle visibly on her face. Out on her own and looking to you less to dictate her feelings, she doesn't always know how to manage and identify the emotions that wash over her. How is she to behave when she feels both relieved and angered by the limits you impose? What words or actions can express her combined sense of excitement and fear as she enters a room full of children she doesn't know?

As an infant, your child's emotional world was a simple one—her contentment or unhappiness depended mainly on her physical state. When her stomach was empty, she wailed with despair. When she was fed, warm, and comforted, she experienced total bliss. As she began to associate these emotions with the adults who helped create them, her emotional life became somewhat more complex. She began actively looking to *you* to respond to her needs, and when you responded, her confidence and emotional ease grew.

Increasingly, the mere fact of your presence or absence influenced your child's emotional state. She felt drawn to experiment with the effects of your disappearances—playing peekaboo as long as you would let her, giggling when you covered her with a blanket and then pretended to "find" her. By age seven to nine months, she was no longer just a cute bundle to be passed easily from person to person. She was quite capable of protesting loudly whenever you left the room. Though she still studied your face for clues to how you—and she—should respond emotionally to events, she had developed her own opinions about how available you should be. As she learned to crawl, her ability to find you in the next room made her feel more confident that she could make physical contact when she needed to. This sense that you were accessible allowed her to explore both her physical and emotional worlds more freely.

The more physically independent your child grew during her second year—crawling, walking, running, and climbing ever farther out of your reach—the more emotionally independent she became as well. For the first time, she let you know that she felt differently from you about some things. "No!" became a powerful new word, and probably her favorite. Though her confidence in using it still depended on how sure she was of your support, she was well on her way to thinking of herself as her own person with her own wishes and goals.

As your toddler approached her second birthday, she may have felt relaxed enough about her physical separation from you to be satisfied with a word or smile, even across an unfamiliar room. When you prepared her ahead of time for the moments when you would leave her with others, she probably became less anxious about such situations. By age two her sense of mastery and numerous drop-offs and pickups have added to her emotional confidence. Having formed a strong attachment to you, she is able to explore the larger world of emotions, relying a bit more on herself for reassurance.

A PARENT'S STORY
"Waaaaaah!"

"My two-year-old, Josh, was watching a videotape of his second birthday party the other day," a teacher at my sons' school told me. "My sister was over, and we were talking, so I wasn't paying much attention to Josh at first. But then I noticed that he got really fascinated at one point in the tape. It was right after the birthday cake part, when Josh grabbed this red balloon off the picnic table and it popped, and Josh started wailing. 'That was sad, wasn't it, Josh?' I said to him. Josh kept staring at the TV screen with an incredibly sad expression on his face.

" 'Josh is sad,' he said to us.

" 'Yes, the balloon popped,' I reminded him while my sister tried not to laugh at his crushed expression. 'But then Daddy gave you a new balloon, remember? Look!' I pointed to the screen, where we could see Josh getting a new balloon. 'Now Josh is happy!'

"I thought that would be the end of it. But instead, Josh turned to us with the same solemn look. 'Wanna see Josh cry,' he demanded. 'Do the tape, Mommy.'

"He seemed really serious about it, so I rewound the tape for him. He watched it again, utterly fascinated—as though he was trying to analyze his 'sadness.' It's just amazing, I think, how many little steps it takes before kids start to understand what's really going on inside."

"HOW DO I FEEL?": EMOTIONAL DEVELOPMENT AT AGE TWO

As an independent two-year-old, your child works hard at providing some of her own emotional needs. She comforts herself when she's anxious and praises herself when she behaves well ("Yay, Casey!"). She even makes an effort to empathize to some extent with those she loves. As she increasingly experiences such new emotions as shame and pride, she grows more interested in the concepts of "good" and "bad" behavior.

Her new autonomy has its downside, too. A two-year-old's most frequently used words at this stage are likely to be "me" and "mine." She may have trouble giving up the spotlight and begin to compete blatantly with siblings for attention. Her realization that she can make things happen makes her *determined* to do so. This willfulness leads to the types of battles for which two-year-olds are well known.

There's no use fighting this period of self-centeredness, since it's just another stage in every child's emotional development. Your two-year-old's will is directly related to her developing sense of self. When this fragile sense is threatened—when she is picked up and set in the bathtub when she's trying to climb into it, or when you give her an apple when she asked for a pear—she dissolves into shrieks of fury not because she's "spoiled" or tired, but because she has lost her hold on her version of the way things are supposed to happen. Later this year, she will more fully understand that others' desires may be as valid as her own. Meanwhile, it's important to mediate between your child and others (pointing out another child's position when yours shouts, "My trike!"), but don't expect your messages to be heard at first. The desire to share, take turns, and otherwise "be nice" comes only after a great deal of cognitive development on her part and patient explanation on yours.

As her cognitive growth continues, increasingly complex emotions and attitudes begin to form within your two-year-old. She will begin to think more about who she is and how she differs from you and others in her world. This self-awareness, along with a greater ability to hold her needs in check, will allow her to experience pride, jealousy, guilt, embarrassment, and misery. Such shadings of emotion, based not on sensory input or on her parents' opinions but on *her own assessment* of her status or behavior, signify a huge step forward in her emotional journey. They add a new layer of depth, making her more interesting in some respects to herself and to others. They also motivate her to continue strengthening her emotional muscles. By the time she celebrates her third birthday, she will have learned how to redirect her negative emotions occasionally into more productive pursuits, such as active physical games or imaginary play. Psychologist Wendy Grolnick and her colleagues showed how this process works by setting children loose in an unfamiliar room filled with toys while their mothers sat nearby, reading or otherwise engaged. At age two, the children weren't very good at adjusting to their mothers' lack of involvement. They called out for their mothers, whined, and clung. By age three, though, they were able to turn away quickly from their mothers and redirect their emotional energy to their play—pretending to be Mommy cooking at the stove and in other ways working out their discomfort through their own activities.

It is impressive how quickly a typical two-year-old learns to recognize, cope with, and even make use of the constant push-pull of her emotional life. Much of the credit for the progress your child has made in managing her emotions this year should go to you. By praising her accomplishments, and by showing satisfaction with your own successes, you have helped her experience the pride born of positive self-evaluation. By working to solve an emotional conflict with your two-year-old instead of just insisting on having your way, you introduced her to the powerful satisfaction of discovering solutions by herself. By empathizing with and helping both your child and others, you reminded her that her own needs aren't the only important ones. And by putting her feelings into words when she couldn't express them herself ("You're mad at Mommy, aren't you? But I know you still love her"), you gave her a giant head start in her efforts to understand what makes herself and others tick.

With this strong beginning, your two-year-old will turn three with a more mature awareness of others' emotions and a greater sensitivity to their feelings. Though she won't always be able to control her emotions, understand what she feels, or be willing to compromise, she will certainly be much further along than she was twelve months ago. As she grows, your continued praise and support will help her learn to judge herself as gently but fairly as you have—and to extend her kindness to others.

"I Didn't Do It!"

Q: My thirty-month-old, Angie, went trick-or-treating for the first time this Halloween and was thrilled to bring home a bag full of candy. Most of the candy was still there the next morning, and Angie wanted to eat some first thing when she got up. We told her she had to wait until after breakfast and sat her down at the table. Instead of obeying us, she waited until both adults were out of the room, then took the candy under the breakfast table and started gobbling it down. When we came back in the room, she quickly stood up straighter so she was better hidden behind the tablecloth. (I guess she didn't realize we could see her anyway.) "Angie, are you eating the candy?" my husband asked. With her mouth full of chocolate, she answered, "No." I was very upset by this obvious lying, but my husband says it's just a stage. Is it something to worry about?

A: Clearly, Angie has reached the point at which she knows she has violated a rule of behavior and feels anxiety over the fact that she's done something wrong. Since she doesn't yet know how to cope with that uncomfortable feeling, she tries to get rid of it. In this case, the first way that occurred to her was to hide. When that failed, the next stage was to try to deny her wrong doing. Your husband is right when he points out that this isn't adult-type fibbing. Angie doesn't yet understand that she's "lying" in the sense that we understand it. She knows only that she feels uncomfortable, and that she can feel less anxious through her untruthful words. No doubt, she also wants to escape the consequences of having disobeyed you.

The way to ensure that her lying remains "only a stage" is to treat it as a lesson in problem-solving. Luckily, at this age kids are terrible liars, so it is usually easy to catch them in mid-lie and deal with the behavior immediately. The best way to do this is to first "name" the situation for your child ("Daddy sees that candy in your mouth. He's sad that you disobeyed"). Repeatedly and patiently, show her how to deal with the discomfort of having disobeyed by telling the truth ("Daddy knows it's hard to behave every time. But when I ask you a question, I want you to tell me what really happened. I won't be too mad if you tell me the truth"). Keep in mind that experiments with lying are bound to happen as any young child grows and learns. What's important now is to help your child learn better ways to cope with a guilty conscience.

"THIS IS ME": BUILDING A PERSONALITY

"I do it!" "I go upstairs!" "I want grapes, please." "Look, I catched it!" Sometimes it seems as though all we hear from our younger two-year-olds is "I, I, I," and "me, me, me." Marching through the house, narrating their actions under their breath, they are completely enthralled by the exciting drama of being themselves. And no wonder—if it's fascinating to us to watch their personalities emerge from the amorphous behavior of babyhood, it must be even more enthralling to them. Suddenly your child realizes that she doesn't like pizza even though her brother does. She nods self-importantly when you point out that Sarah hasn't yet learned to share as well as she. She attempts a new activity and, depending on how much freedom she's given to pursue it, learns a little or a lot about herself in the process.

Of course, your child has been receiving information about herself

Age two opens up a wide range of emotions as your child's unique personality blooms.

since infancy. Your care and constant presence told her how valuable a person she was. Your willingness to let her toddle away while you kept watch let her know that she was a capable, active individual. If she was uncertain about your emotional availability during those years, she may have at least temporarily become more anxious and less adventurous. Now, however, as she begins to define herself somewhat less by your responses to her and more by her own criteria, her ability to explore independently is bringing her to a fuller knowledge of her strengths and weaknesses.

The person who emerges will not necessarily be the person you expect. To some degree, your child possesses a basic, inherited temperament that makes her simply "who she is." She may have been born with a high or low activity level, a sociable or shy nature, a sensitive or generally easygoing response to change, and marked difficulty or relative ease in handling emotional stress. Another important element in your toddler's development is how well her temperament matches your own. If you're a reclusive person who likes to stay at home reading a book on a Saturday night, you probably don't enjoy your sociable child's constant efforts to chat with strangers when the two of you are out and about. When she refuses to stay by your side and instead runs off after another child to strike up a conversation, you may decide she's "rebellious" by nature when in fact she's simply different from you. Your negative feelings about her may set up a negative cycle in which each of you insists on behaving in your own way, instead of recognizing that neither way is the only "right way." One key to successful parenting lies in choosing techniques that suit your particular type of child. Studies have shown that very active toddlers play more competently when their mothers don't intervene much, while less active toddlers benefit when their mothers are actively involved in their play. Likewise, a shy two-year-old might prefer to develop her strengths in the quiet of her own home, while a sociable child learns best from her peers. Clearly, you cannot encourage your child's optimal development simply by following generic instructions laid out by parenting experts. Instead, you need to observe your child's particular responses to a variety of techniques and then settle on the approaches that bring out the best in her.

As your child moves through the first months of her third year, she will grow increasingly aware of the many "I's" she can be: the angry "I," the affectionate "I," the good "I," the naughty "I." What she doesn't yet understand is that all of these "I's" are contemporaneously part of one person—just as *you* can be the loving parent, the impatient parent, and the tired parent all at once. Though she has a sense that she is a person who carries out actions from one moment to another ("I climb the stairs," "I give the apple to Daddy"), she does not really comprehend the fact that she can hold many different emotions inside of her and still be the same person. She can be both an angry girl and a loving girl.

Several months of cognitive and verbal development must pass before your child can come to terms with her emotional fluctuations. At some point around the middle of the year, she will make her first connections between how she feels at one moment and how she feels the next. Gradually, she will begin to compare her past behaviors and ponder the advantages of one over the other in a particular situation. She will experiment with a variety of expressions in her pretend play and compare her own emotional expressions to those of her peers, her parents, and even characters on TV. She will enjoy imitating a variety of attitudes ("I'm strong! I'm Supergirl!") in the process of figuring out which ones suit her best. As she approaches age three, her urge to explore her emotional range may even lead her to fake her emotions— by pretending to cry when someone takes away a toy, or by pouting, teasing, or showing affection to get what she wants. This primitive form of emotional manipulation is a normal part of her development. She will soon learn from your consistent responses which emotional ploys are acceptable and which are not.

Responding supportively and consistently to your two-year-old provides her with an important emotional anchor. As your child swings from one mood to another, terrified one moment, furious the next, and full of affection a moment later, she may easily wonder just where in this emotional chaos she is. At twenty-four months, the experience of feeling more than one emotion at once ("I want to be a good girl. I want to be mean. Grrr!") can be frightening and confusing. Your ability to verbalize what she feels ("It's hard to share ice cream when we want it all ourselves") grounds her and restores her to a sense of constancy. As this feeling of constancy grows stronger—as she learns that even when she loses emotional control and acts out, you will remain there for her—her sense of self-constancy will grow. Eventually, at around age three, she will begin to understand that her self endures despite temporary glitches in relationships—that while her emotions are fleeting, the essential *her* stays the same. As her self-perception stabilizes, her behavior will grow more consistent. You, too, will begin to notice certain behavioral patterns and personality traits that may remain beyond this year. Saying good-bye to the simplicity of your child's babyhood is certainly sad in some respects, but you will be rewarded with new, almost daily discoveries about her developing self. Though there is still a great deal of room for change, by the time she turns three the essence of her personality is visible for all to see.

THE TOY BOX
At Thirty Months

Hunter has been having a grand time with the toys in his toy box while Mom is on the phone. He's spread them all over the family room and down the hall, and he's currently lugging a bag of blocks to set up in the kitchen. Just then a voice cries out from behind him, "Hunter Jackson! What on earth!" Hunter freezes in his tracks. *It's Mom!*

"Hunter, you know better than to make a mess like this. Come here right now. We're going to clean it up."

"I wanna play blocks," Hunter informs her, holding up his bag of blocks.

"I don't care what you want to do. This is a disaster!" Mommy says in her no-nonsense tone as she starts to clean. "We have company coming tonight."

"But, Mom." Hunter's shoulders droop. The bag of blocks

dangles listlessly from one hand. "I wanna play blocks," he says in a tiny voice. When his mother looks up at him, he makes his chin quiver. "Waaaaaaaaaaah!" he wails.

His mother shakes her head, stifling a laugh. She's very annoyed, but Hunter's crying act is so fake it's funny. "That's not going to work on me, kid," she says briskly, taking the bag of blocks from him and adding it to her pile of toys. "Come on now. First, help me clean up, and then I'll make you an ice cream cone."

Hunter hesitates. *Ice cream is nice,* he thinks. The crying act didn't work this time. But cleaning up usually makes Mom happy. With a sigh, he squats down and picks up a toy.

"DON'T LET HIM GET ME!": ANXIETY AND FEAR

"On the day we decided to adopt Letty, Barbara and I agreed there would be no secrets in our family," Letty's father, Dan, told me during an interview. "We planned to let her know she was adopted as soon as she could understand what that meant, and to tell her all we knew about her biological parents. Around the time she turned two, though, we started to have second thoughts. All kinds of fears seemed to surface then—not just a fear of the dark and stuff like that, but getting scared about whether we *loved* her whenever we got mad! I started to wonder whether she had these anxieties because she sensed somehow that we weren't her "first" parents—I guess most adoptive parents worry about that. Anyway, our concerns about her nightmares and fears scared us enough that we avoided even mentioning anything to do with adoption. We even stopped reading children's books with characters who didn't have parents. Looking back, I wonder if it was our own anxiety that was making Letty uneasy. I think now that it probably made things worse. If I had it to do over again, I'd definitely go back to the original plan—treating the subject in an honest, relaxed way, and dealing with our own discomfort before we looked for hers."

Of course, adopted children aren't the only ones who experience anxiety and even fear this year. Having largely mastered their movement skills and made excellent progress in language, two-year-olds are primed to look around with a more sophisticated eye at their social and emotional environment—and as any parent of a child this age will tell you, they pick up on nearly everything. For the first time, they not only notice but *think about* the fact that Mommy or Daddy looks sad today. They link the image of water draining out of the bathtub with the possibility of swirling down the drain themselves. They peer at the shadows in their room at night and see strange shapes in the darkness. And it's possible that a parent's discomfort about a particular topic (whether adoption, as in Letty's case, or household finances, or anything else) might spark some fear or anxiety.

On the one hand, these new thoughts and feelings are an encouraging sign that your child's imagination is developing right on schedule. On the other hand, certain fears and anxieties can disrupt her sleep routines, social interactions, and general attitude. As you try to deal with these negative feelings keep in mind that, though her fears may seem irrational to you, they are very real to her. She has used her very limited reasoning abilities to arrive at what seem to be logical conclusions—and your brusque assurances ("There's no way the ogre in the book can get you," or, "You know Mommy doesn't leave you at the sitter's overnight") don't convince her that she's wrong. For this reason, it's important to listen carefully to your child's descriptions of her fears so as to pinpoint the source of her anxiety. Once you understand that she's terrified of masks because she thinks they're alive, you can touch one for her, drop it on the ground, encourage her to touch it herself, and otherwise demonstrate that it's inanimate. Once you learn that she's afraid of the dark because a shadow in her room looks like a monster, you can switch the light on and off, showing her what makes the shadow, close the closet door, or install a night-light. When you realize that she's experiencing a meltdown because you punished her for a misdeed and she thinks you've stopped loving her altogether, you can explain that you were angry for only a minute. Listening to your child and carefully clarifying matters for her will reassure her much more than a command to "stop being such a baby," ignoring her fears, or encouraging her to overcome them on her own. Keep in mind that negative feelings are natural counterparts to positive ones. They're part of life—and this year she needs your help in learning to manage them.

Not all fears are based on a child's misunderstandings. Your child may experience anxiety over the death or departure of a loved one or conflict within her family. As Dan suspected regarding his adopted two-year-old, avoiding these issues does nothing to ease your child's discomfort. They can be dealt with only through repeated conversations—held at the child's level of comprehension—in which you try to clear up your child's misunderstandings, identify and discuss real dangers, and help her express how they make her feel. Children's stories that address such fears can be helpful, as can your willingness to work out these issues through play. Gradually, through such efforts, your child will come to understand that, while fears come and go, you are always there to support and protect her. You will have not only put her mind at ease but added another layer of support to her emotional base.

IF YOU'RE CONCERNED
Coping with Anxiety

Hobbled by limited reasoning powers and a frequent inability to express their fears, two-year-olds often find themselves in a position of knowing just enough to feel anxious, but not enough to be able to reassure themselves. Such triggers as a parent's frequent absence (particularly when it's not explained), discord within the family, the arrival of a new sibling, or even a parent's overprotectiveness can cause a young child to withdraw physically or emotionally from her parents or her environment, to behave aggressively, or to dissolve into overexcited shrieks and giggles. These defense mechanisms take the place of words for the child, allowing her to express her feelings and signal her need for help.

As with simpler fears, the best way to respond to such anxious behavior is to show your child that you are there to support her and to search gently—through conversation and play—for the cause of her discomfort. Once you understand why she has withdrawn or otherwise behaved defensively, you can correct any errors she's made in interpreting events. If your child fights you off when you arrive to pick her up at the sitter's, as Megan did at the beginning of this chapter, first clarify whether she's simply having a lot of fun. If she behaves the same way consistently from day to day, consider why she's so angry and defensive. Sometimes such feelings are not caused by any real events but are brought on when a child senses a parent's ambivalence. If you feel guilty about leaving your child in someone else's care, she will probably pick up on your worry that you've "abandoned" her. If you or your partner resent the balance of child-care responsibility in your marriage, your child may internalize your resentment and express it through her behavior.

In other words, your child's anxiety may be an expression of erroneous assumptions that you can clear up with sensitivity and patience—or it may result from very real emotions and situations that threaten her sense of safety. If you cannot change the negative factors in your child's world, or the emotional atmosphere that causes her discomfort, it may be necessary to consult a professional. A sense of safety is the most essential element in a young child's development. If your child's behavior reflects a belief that she has no one to depend on, it's better to get help for her sooner rather than later.

"GIMME THAT!":
ACTS OF AGGRESSION

Overwhelmed by conflicting emotions, unable to fully understand what's going on around them and still limited in their ability to share, take turns, and postpone gratification, two-year-olds sometimes, understandably, express their frustration in physical ways. As they begin to interact with others their age, their aggressive behavior can become more of an issue. No parent likes to see his child hit or bite a playmate, and certainly no child wants to play with someone who frequently hits or bites. Factors that tend to increase aggressive behavior—family stress (a new baby), physical stress (not enough sleep the night before), or even the relative sizes of the children (the aggressor simply being bigger and stronger than her playmate)—seem beside the point when you are apologizing to your child's friend or the friend's parent.

The bad news is that there is likely to be a great deal of aggression in your child's life this year—whether it's instigated by her or the children with whom she plays. The good news is that physical aggression typically decreases over time as your child learns to curb her impulsiveness and finds other ways to handle conflicts, such as negotiation. In the meantime, it may comfort you to know that her impulsive smack on the arm of a friend isn't a deliberate attempt to hurt him—it's just that she *must* have the toy he's holding and can't make herself wait for him to let it go. According to a 1992 study by Deborah Vandell of the University of Texas and and her colleague Mark Bailey, "property disputes" occur every five minutes among two-and-a-half-year-olds. Practically all of the aggression that two-year-olds practice against one another centers on objects. Though they are old enough to know that hurting other people is bad and will bring disapproval their way, they aren't far enough along cognitively to hurt another child deliberately.

Learning to control aggression is all about learning to think before acting. Your child's ability to control frustration, delay gratification, and work out tension in more positive ways will increase naturally to some extent as her cognitive growth continues. Certainly, she will need your support a great deal as she weathers the two-year-old's typical storms of intense, if fleeting, anger. You will need to explain to her—calmly and repeatedly—why grabbing, hitting, or biting is never a good idea. You will need to show her how to employ her developing language skills, to "use her words" instead of her body. (Older siblings provide a wonderful, natural context in which to teach these lessons.) When no one is getting hurt, it's fine to let disputes between two-year-olds work themselves out. By solving conflicts on their own, children learn valuable skills for the next time and gain experience in delaying gratification as well. But keep a vigilant eye on fights in the making. It is in no way a positive, instructive experience for a two-year-old to hit a child and then be punished for it. In fact, allowing her to act aggressively and then "pay the consequences" only sets up a pattern of behavior that can be difficult for her to break. The best way to deal with her aggression is to anticipate situations that might create frustration and do your best to help her avoid them.

One way to prevent aggressive behavior before it happens is to limit the amount of aggression to which your child is exposed every day. The media are saturated with images, talk, and reportage of violent acts. According to a 1996 study commissioned by Mediascope, 57 percent of all television programs aired between 6:00 A.M. and 11:00 P.M. contain violent scenes—but 66 *percent* of children's programs do. Keep in mind that most children aged two to three watch about an hour and a half of television a day. As your two-year-old's awareness of her environment expands, she will mimic and experiment with the aggressive behavior she sees at the movies or on TV. You don't have to unplug the radio and throw away the VCR, but you do need to be vigilant. Your child is learning from what she hears and sees.

It's also important to take note of your child's "triggers"—the kinds of situations that frequently lead her to behave aggressively. Many two-year-olds dissolve into kicks and screams much more easily when they're tired. Yours may also become easily overstimulated by crowds and respond to being dropped into the middle of a birthday party by hitting the other guests. Two-year-olds who aren't ready to share valued possessions (and most of them aren't) will probably hurt another child to get an object they want. Active children who resent being confined may strike out at those who try to pick them up and hold them. Once you have familiarized yourself with these causes of aggression, you can easily avoid a great many of them. It isn't necessary to force your two-year-old to deal with a crowd of kids if she isn't ready, for example. Your child will fare better (and so will you) if you stay by her side and help her initiate some play with another child. If she tends to grow more aggressive when she's overstimulated or tired, make a point of letting her nap before a stressful activity (including those she enjoys), and give her a brief break from the action when you see her begin to lose control. Spread events out over a day or week to prevent burnout and loss of control. Resist the temptation to leave your two-year-old unsupervised for long just because she's old enough not to need your constant help. (She's not quite ready to play peacefully on her own.) Watch her even more closely when younger or smaller children are present. And be sure to set a good example yourself of positive ways to deal with anger and frustration.

As the months pass and your two-year-old gains more experience in what constitutes good behavior—and as her sense of herself as a consistently "good" girl takes root in the latter half of the year—she will be better able to tolerate frustration and rechannel her aggressive impulses. Gradually her defiant kicks and shouts will recede as she learns, with your support and patience, to manage the frustration of being asked to do something she doesn't want to do and to wait a bit for what she wants. Your good example will go a long way in demonstrating the rewards of good behavior. The next time a telephone salesperson interrupts the family dinner, don't slam down the phone. Smile for your observant two-year-old's benefit, politely end the conversation, and get back to your meal.

EASING THE WAY
When Your Child Strikes Out

We all have our bad days, and your two-year-old is no exception. When she responds to a buildup of frustration by hitting you or biting another child, remind yourself that this is just a sign of how limited her emotional resources still are, and certainly not a sign that she is "bad." To help your child recover and teach her that such behavior will not serve her well, avoid giving her an audience during her tirade. Instead, control your (perfectly natural) impulse to scream back and, if necessary, step away until you've regained control, allowing another adult to deal with her. When you feel better able to control your own aggression, state briefly what you think she's feeling ("I understand that you're mad because I want you to brush your teeth"). Then tell her why she can't respond aggressively ("But you can't hit people just because they make you mad. It hurts them. In this family, we don't hurt people"). Be sure your tone of voice conveys your conviction that this is important. She will pick up on any wavering or lack of confidence and instinctively exploit it.

Once you've acknowledged the reason for her behavior and reminded her that it's still unacceptable, give her a likable alternative if possible ("How about if we try the slides for a change? I haven't seen you slide in a long time"). You might distract her ("As soon as we leave, we can watch your new video"). If all else fails, humor usually works ("Is that an elephant on the playground? Let's go see!"). Sometimes simply giving her an extra moment to collect herself will get her back on track. Sometimes you may benefit from taking a brief time-out yourself.

There are times, however, when your child will simply be unable to stop her aggression. You may have to pick her up and put her in a place where she can work out her anger. Two-year-olds greatly resent giving up control of their bodies, and she will no doubt scream and kick as you carry her away, but don't be dissuaded. She needs the chance to calm down. Keep in mind that threats or comments aimed at inducing fear or guilt ("How could you be so bad?") are not only cruel but counterproductive. Likewise, general statements such as, "You have to share," and, "Hey now, be good!" only overwhelm and confuse her. Instead,

There will be times when your two-year-old's behavior will shock or embarrass you. Take heart—you're not alone!

tell her specifically what you want her to do, as in, "Let go of David's arm. It's his turn to throw the ball."

Once your child is calmer, it's a good idea to review briefly what happened with her. (The car ride home is a good time to talk, because she's confined and separated from distractions.) If you can put her feelings into words, she will feel supported and relieved. Your understanding can put the experience in perspective and help her use it to teach herself where she went wrong and how she might behave in more positive ways next time.

Finally, give your child a hug before sending her back into the fray. Her aggressive behavior is at least as upsetting to her as it is to you, and it's important for her to know that, though you don't approve of her aggressive behavior, you do approve of her. A quick signal of affection won't erase what you have said—it will only emphasize the fact that she is supported and loved even when she makes mistakes.

"I MISSED YOU TODAY!": LEARNING TO SHARE EMOTIONS

Nearly a year has passed, and Marjorie's life has settled down a bit. She and Nick have formally divorced and agreed on a custody arrangement that satisfies them both. Marjorie has weathered the layoffs at work and managed to hold on to her job. As the stresses in her life have diminished somewhat, she has been able to step back and see Megan's behavior not as just another overwhelming problem to deal with, and not as something directed purposefully at her, but as a young child's expression of her own anxiety and fear.

Today, as Marjorie climbs the steps to the baby-sitter's front door, she knows that Megan may not be eager to leave at first. Not only does Megan enjoy her time at the sitter's, but, as Marjorie has learned over the past months, she is simply by temperament not a person who makes transitions easily. At home Marjorie has learned that giving

Megan a "countdown" before a new activity makes an enormous difference in her behavior. When Megan knows that "in ten minutes we'll be leaving," then "in five minutes," then "in one minute," she is reasonably ready to put her coat on by the time Marjorie is ready to go out the door.

Marjorie has also come to understand that Megan's screams ("Go away! I don't want you!") were the only way she could express her anxiety over all the changes in her life. Not only was her vocabulary still very limited, but Megan wasn't yet old enough at twenty-four or thirty months to understand her feelings. Marjorie's own ambivalence about hiring a sitter was another major factor in Megan's discomfort, Marjorie realizes now. Even when children can't identify a parent's emotion, they often pick up on it. Only after months of patient conversation, storytelling, and even compromise, when possible, has Megan begun to adjust to things as they are now.

"Come on in," Catherine says to Marjorie when she answers the door. "Megan's just finishing a picture she drew for you. It's really nice!"

"Hi, sweetie," Marjorie calls to her daughter as she steps inside. "How are you? I missed you today."

"Don't want to go," Megan responds, keeping her eyes on her work. Six months ago, these words would have devastated Marjorie and led her to question yet again her decision to work outside the home. Now, Marjorie takes them in stride. Why should Megan want to leave this instant, after all, when she's right in the middle of a project?

"Okay, you finish your picture," Marjorie says, sitting at the table near her daughter. "I'll talk to Catherine about your day, and when you're finished, we'll go home. Five minutes, okay?"

Megan doesn't answer, but Marjorie sees her relax a bit as she continues her drawing. She smiles, relieved to have avoided a crisis. "So," she says, turning to Catherine, "what kind of fun did you guys have?"

With luck and a great deal of effort, you, too, will see improvement this year in the way your moods and emotions mesh with your child's. As the two of you experiment with ways to express your emotions in positive ways, to meet each other's expectations much of the time, and to find productive means of dealing with the times you don't, you will find your daily life together proceeding much more smoothly. You will show your two-year-old consistently that there are limits beyond which you will not allow her to go, and that you are there to support her as she works to conform to those limits. In time, she will gain in self-confidence and courage to explore, and her emotional states will stabilize. With your help, she will come to appreciate the value of compromise and creative problem-solving, and she will learn that problems can be solved and despair is temporary. Best of all, as she approaches her preschool years, she will begin to internalize these lessons, and they will continue to support her emotional development as she establishes a life outside her home.

ADVANCES
Emotional Achievements in the Third Year

24 MONTHS	Self-confidence has increased
	Thrives on a reliable routine
	Can be bossy at times
	Takes pride in doing things herself
27 MONTHS	May experience frequent mood swings
	May begin to feel guilt when caught misbehaving
	Can sometimes express sadness or anxiety
30 MONTHS	May resent surrendering spotlight to siblings or peers
	Behavior is generally less impulsive
	May enjoy trying out different emotional expressions
33 MONTHS	Becomes curious about other people's moods

36 MONTHS   May show sympathy to those she loves

Expresses affection spontaneously

FIRST-PERSON SINGULAR

Your child may be particularly interested in reading the notes you make here once she's grown old enough to wonder about her early development. She will probably want to know what her earliest fears and passions were, and how she first learned to deal with the frustrations of everyday life. Be sure to record any incidents in which she went out of her way to make another person feel better. She will need to know later that, while she was oftentimes moody, she was generally a very kind and generous child.

READER'S NOTES

_____

_____

_____

_____

_____

_____

_____

_____

_____

"Play with Me!"—
My Social Development

Your child's developing awareness of the world around him will increase his ability to consider others' feelings and to want them to be happy.

"Come in!" Eileen says to twenty-four-month-old Jeff and his mother, Mary, as she steps back to let them pass into the living room. Eileen's twenty-six-month-old, Noel, sits on the living room floor beside his toy basket, playing with a wooden train set. "Look, Jeff," Eileen says to their visitor. "Noel's playing trains. Want to join him?"

Eileen has looked forward to this first play date between her son and Jeff, who met at a mutual friend's second birthday party. Eileen and Mary hit it off immediately, and the boys shared a great deal of enthusiasm for the helium balloons. Eileen hopes Jeff will turn into a regular playmate for her son, who has two older sisters but doesn't get many chances to play with kids his age.

"Jeff, say hi to Noel's mom," Mary prompts her son, but Jeff just marches past her toward the toy basket. Mary and Eileen glance at each other and laugh. *Who cares about parents,* the boys must be thinking, *when there's another guy to hang out with?*

"Would you like some coffee?" Eileen asks Mary as Jeff settles down on the floor near Noel. "I've just made a pot." Mary follows her into the kitchen, leaving the two-year-olds to play side by side. As she pours the coffee, Eileen begins asking Mary some of the questions she's saved up for this play date: how their visit to a local preschool went, how long they've been in the neighborhood, what other stay-at-home moms she's met so far, and how she likes living in this city. They are deep in conversation when a scream issues from the living room: "*My car! Give that back!*" Noel shouts.

Both mothers rush to the living room, where they find Noel up on his feet, in a rage. Jeff stands near him, clutching a toy car close to his chest and closing his eyes to withstand Noel's assault. To Eileen's horror, Noel raises his fist, which still holds a wooden train engine, and brings the engine crashing down on Jeff's head. "Give me that car!" he shouts, and then gives a shriek of utter frustration that Eileen recognizes from his constant bouts with his sisters.

Eileen rushes to pull her son off of his guest. Jeff collapses, wailing, into his mother's arms. *Well, there we go,* Eileen thinks glumly as each mother tries to bring her son back into a reasonable frame of mind. *They'll never come over here again. Noel's so used to defending himself against his older sisters. He really needs to learn how to behave with kids his age—but if he hits and yells at them when they come to visit, how will he ever get the chance to learn?*

As exciting a time as this third year is for your child's social growth, it is also a year of very bumpy progress. These uneven periods, or "touchpoints," as my colleague Dr. T. Berry Brazelton describes them, involve great leaps in social ability followed by bewildering periods of regression. Parents of a verbally adept two-year-old may feel especially confident that their child understands how to interact successfully with others—only to find that he uses his many words to do battle with a potential playmate. Nothing is more discouraging than watching your young two-year-old, who says "please" and "thank you" to adults so sweetly when reminded, turn into a shouting, aggressive, and completely graceless child when you try to introduce him to a new playmate. Social skills are not innate, however, nor do they develop automatically alongside language and cognitive abilities. Your two-year-old must be taught how to behave with adults and with other children, and he must practice carrying out your instructions over and over. Finally, he must want to make deeper connections with people other than his caretakers—a desire that manifests itself only after other growth occurs.

In this chapter, we will see how a two-year-old's focus moves gradually from objects to other people, how he becomes increasingly aware that another person's point of view may differ from his own, and how he uses his interactions with others to experiment with social behavior and decide which types work best for him. A twenty-four-month-old may demonstrate his sociable tendencies by showing a caregiver an object he has found. By showing his discovery to her, he not only informs her about the object but shares his excitement about it. As he grows older, he may move from sharing or tussling over objects with a child his age to playing side by side at the same activity, and finally perhaps to "playing pretend" with him. His experience of the other child's habits, behavior, and expressions of emotion will teach him a great deal about the variety of social tools available to everyone and bring him that much further along in his social development.

As your child's ability to observe and analyze such actions improves this year, along with his skill at maintaining a sequence of social behavior ("thank you" follows "please"), he will no longer become so easily overwhelmed by glitches in his interaction with others. Rather than erupt in a rage when another child frustrates his desires, he will begin to use one of a number of social tools with which you and others have equipped him ("I'll take green. You have this one"). He will draw on an increasing ability to delay gratification, and he may even realize that the other child holds a valid point of view. Of course, his social life won't always be rosy, but if you give him patience, support, and a few well-placed instructions, he'll soon learn to maneuver through the conflicting desires that constitute a social existence. His eagerness to master this new skill will show in his eyes when, after playing for half an hour with a child he's just met, he announces, "I made a *friend!*"—though he probably hasn't even learned her name.

First Friends

"I started back to work part-time just a couple of months after Allison turned one," a mother told me while we were waiting for our kids to be released from their gymnastics class. "My neighbor had a two-year-old child, Ruby, who was cared for by a full-time nanny, and she and the nanny offered to have Allison stay with Ruby while I was at work. My neighbor had this whole fantasy about Ruby and Allison becoming best friends. I didn't see it, frankly, since the girls were six months apart in age, but I needed the child care so I went along with it.

"At first, it worked out just about as I had expected. It seemed like every time I went to pick Allison up, she and Ruby were screaming because one had hit the other or taken the other's toy or some such thing. Even when they were playing quietly, they didn't really play *together.* It was more like they'd play with different toys in the same room, mostly ignoring each other.

"Now that Allison's nearly three, though, I'm starting to think that my neighbor was right after all. The girls really do seem to be becoming friends of a sort. When they have a fight, they seem to be able to work it out faster than Allison can with other kids. And they cooperate a lot more. They have their little games that they play over and over, and they both know all the rules. The best part is, Allison seems to have picked up a lot of behavior tips from Ruby over the past year. Once Ruby figures out how to say, "I'm sorry," she makes sure Allison learns, too. Of course, she still doesn't want to let Allison be the doctor instead of the patient when they play hospi-

148 | WATCH ME GROW: I'M TWO

tal, but at least Allison has learned how to insist that they take turns."

"I WANT A FRIEND": SOCIAL GROWTH IN THE FIRST THREE YEARS

Of all the abilities that young children develop during their early years, social skills are perhaps the ones we parents most take for granted—and most misunderstand. Moms and dads who would naturally dismiss the idea of, say, trying to teach a three-month-old to talk, frequently meet in "play groups" where they expect their infants to acknowledge and enjoy one another. These types of get-togethers are wonderful for parents and may even benefit the babies indirectly as their parents exchange valuable information and necessary empathy. Infants, however, are necessarily focused on their own inner sensations and experiences and aren't yet cognitively advanced enough to enjoy playing with others their age. A baby must first learn that he has hands, feet, and a powerful voice before he can use them to meet, greet, and explore the world.

Since babies can't tell us what they know and don't know, it's difficult to judge exactly when they first become aware that they are separate beings in a social setting, rather than a part of their mothers and the rest of their environment. Certainly, your child's new ability to crawl between six and nine months of age led to more encounters with people and objects and thus gave him more experience of his separateness. At age one, his use of words to label objects helped him distinguish himself even more—demonstrating his understanding that a "doggie" was different from "me." As his social thinking grew more complex, he gradually began to comprehend the fact that others were not only physically separate from him but emotionally and mentally separate as well. He realized the two of you might respond completely differently to an event and would know how the other felt only if you communicated your feelings in some way. Few revelations are as mind-boggling as this one to a toddler. Your child no doubt revealed his interest through a process called *social referencing*—checking your responses to actions you both witnessed (another child crying for a bottle) and to his own actions (throwing his cereal bowl on the floor). By eighteen months, your child understood that the images of babies he saw on television were not images of himself—and that the person in the mirror *was* his own reflection. He had become sufficiently aware of his social surroundings to point out objects only if someone was there to see and hear him—instead of pointing and gesturing even when he was alone, as younger infants do.

It's easy to mistake the eighteen-month-old's awareness of others as a readiness to play with kids his age. But even the apparently natural desire to socialize requires several more developmental steps before it can be realized. The skills needed for play—taking turns, listening, empathizing, co-creating—are beyond the range of a toddler with limited language abilities and intense self-focus. Though your child was probably content to be placed in a room with another toddler, and enjoyed watching and even mimicking him, it's unlikely that the two children fully interacted. At age one, you and his other caregivers still instigated most of your toddler's social growth—teaching him verbal formulas ("Hi," "Bye-bye," "I'm sorry"), helping him find acceptable ways to communicate his feelings ("Don't whine, Troy, use your words"), and demonstrating the rhythms and body language of everyday conversation.

By now, however, your two-year-old has probably mastered the basics well enough to interact in more satisfying ways with other children as well as adults. His interest in others' emotions motivates him to reach out, while his great leaps in language ability make social interaction much easier. Now he truly enjoys the play dates you arrange for him, particularly if he's known the other child for a while. As the year unfolds, he will express a desire to share his experience with this child, saying, "Did you see that?" when he does something amazing, such as drop a ball through a basket. His increased memory will allow him to think and talk about his playmates when they aren't present ("Clara likes frogs"), and his growing cognitive abilities will allow him to learn even more from them through imitation ("I hop like Mikey!"). He and his playmates may well continue to play side by side rather than together—and his emotional needs may make it hard for him to give up the spotlight to someone else—but with your encouragement and specific prompting ("Why don't we build a sandcastle together?"), he will begin to learn how to play *with,* rather than *beside,* a sibling or another child. Participation in group day care or nursery school will give him even more experience in this area. In fact, these encounters with nonfamily members can have a great impact on his social development. Studies have shown that a young child's general adjustment, competence with peers, and complexity of play are related to the quality of child care he is given and to his relationships with caregivers.

By his third birthday, your child's social world will have expanded immensely. He will have become conscious of and interested in a wide variety of adults and children he hardly noticed before. Now when you get together with a group of parents and their three-year-olds, you may enjoy the sight of two or more children playing together in the way we usually imagine. Of course, three-year-olds still often have a hard time sharing, listening, and acknowledging another child's desires, but with your patient tutelage, your child will have learned to enjoy playing hide-and-seek, chase, and "pretend" with others. He'll have begun to understand that the child he's playing with is not an obstacle but a *friend.* And he may even have learned to share the spotlight—though this will be harder at some times than at others.

THE TOY BOX
At Thirty-two Months

The entire family is watching a movie on television, and two-year-old Cam is bored. He wanders over to his toy box in the living room and rummages around, looking for something to do. Suddenly he spots his sword—the beautiful gray plastic sword his uncle gave him for his birthday. That sword has been the center of a great deal of dramatic play among Cam and his three siblings—all boys. Gazing at it, Cam remembers wonderful battles in the backyard, in the basement, and racing from bedroom to bedroom upstairs.

"Look out!" Cam shouts, grabbing the sword and raising it high over his head, just as his older brother James does. Instantly his three older brothers turn to look at him. Basking in the attention, Cam jumps forward, waving the sword. "Look out!" he crows.

As his parents laugh, two of Cam's brothers leap up and grab the sword from him. "En garde!" the older one shouts, jumping onto the back of an easy chair. "Henry, stop that right now!" his dad shouts as Henry races across the living room, two brothers in tow.

Cam stands, arms at his side, staring after his brothers. Everyone was looking at him—and now they're not! Now they're looking at *Henry,* and Henry has the sword! Cam feels a wave of despair wash over him. He tried to make something interesting happen. Something is happening, all right, but it doesn't have anything to do with him. Frustrated and helpless to change the course of events, he begins to wail. Even when his dad comes to comfort him—even when he orders Henry to give back the sword—Cam has a hard time recovering his equilibrium. Even after his brothers have turned back to the movie, he continues sniffling, wiping his face with his sleeve. *He* wants to control what happens with his toys! *He* wants to direct the play! He clutches his sword close. Next time he won't let them take it away.

"SAY HELLO": TEACHING YOUR CHILD THE RULES OF SOCIAL INTERACTION

"I have to admit, sometimes I long for the good old days," a friend remarked as we picked our kids up from preschool. "I remember when all I had to do to keep Anthony happy was to be there, smiling at him. Now that he can talk, it's, 'Let's go outside,' and, 'Gimme!' and, 'I don't *want* to hug Grandma!' all day long. All of a sudden, I have to negotiate every minute of the day. When is this going to end?"

There's no denying that, over the past two or more years, your healthy, inquisitive child has moved steadily away from the more observant state of infancy into the active role of full-fledged member of the family. Whereas initially you, as his parent, did more of the giving and he did more of the taking, your relationship increasingly became a two-way street. The remarkable cognitive, emotional, and verbal growth he achieved by age two enabled him to question your decisions, defy your orders, probe your emotions, and return your expressions of affection. Fortunately, these same advances enabled him to begin to learn the rules of social engagement—from everyone in his environment, but especially from you.

Your child has long been primed to learn from you the best ways of interacting with other people. From his first day of life, when he grasped something, kicked a foot, or performed some other random action, you responded with an eager smile, pleasant sounds, and perhaps a gentle hug. As he grew, he listened to the rhythms of your speech and watched how you approached others in your world. Peekaboo games provided him with early lessons in the turn-taking aspects of social interaction. His constant testing of your responses to his actions led to a steady stream of information on how to respond to similar situations himself.

During his third year, your child begins to express much more freely all that he has learned before. Having tested your responses and compared them to his own for over a year, he is well aware that you (or any other person) may have opinions completely different from his own. So when you offer him an apple, he may remind you that he likes cookies. When you tell him it's bathtime, he may announce (loudly) that he doesn't want to take a bath. This sudden urge to take a stand in his relations with you and others is quite trying for many parents, but at least it's a sign that he is eager to take his place as a member of his society. In fact, an inability to stand up for himself would be cause for concern in a two-year-old. As he enters the wider world, he needs to establish his place.

Your two-year-old is eager not only to achieve full partnership in his interactions with others but to learn the social rules that will best help him reach his goals. This is the year when he will learn whether a scream or a polite request is more likely to get him the TV time he longs for. Now is the time when he will begin to say "Excuse me" as a matter of course—or will deliberately not say it. Though he is still too young to understand *why* he must wait in line, refrain from interrupting, and so on, he is old enough to begin practicing these skills and to understand that it pleases you (and other important adults). As he experiments with your suggestions (saying "Thank you" when an adult offers him a toy, for example, or saying to a child, "Do you want some pizza?") and gets positive results (beaming adults, a happy playmate), he will use them more often. Of course, this progression will not be steady—he will also experiment with less positive ploys and frequently forget the good behaviors he's learned. But your approval and support are very powerful forces in his life this year. The more you reward his efforts at demonstrating correct social behavior, the harder he will try to live up to your expectations.

Another way in which you can encourage your child's social development this year is by acting as an interpreter of other people's emotions and motivations. Your two-year-old is fascinated by others' points of view, yet he often lacks the experience to understand how they feel. He will need many, many reminders this year that "hitting Bobby *hurts* him, just like Bobby's hitting hurts you," and, "People like it when you smile and talk nicely to them. Screaming hurts their ears." Only in this way can he begin to comprehend not only that other people have their own feelings, but that his actions affect those feelings in important ways.

By the second half of this year, your child will have come to rely on you to introduce him to the rules of social interaction and to explain why we behave toward one another as we do. Not all of these lessons will have been directly stated. You will have familiarized him with the practice of turn-taking by playing simple games with him, taught him the importance of reciprocity by completing chores together, and instilled a rudimentary respect for others' opinions through your casual, daily conversations.

It's important to keep in mind this year, especially when your two-year-old is misbehaving in public, that children don't instinctively understand even the basic rules of social interaction. Acceptable behavior springs almost entirely from the instructions and example that you and others give him, this year and in the years to come. As your child learns to shape his natural impulses in ways that better suit his interactions with others, he will gain a better sense of where he stands in his environment. He will possess, if not always act on, a greater understanding of what makes relationships proceed more smoothly. He will have learned to respect his own opinions, and sometimes even to respect yours.

A CHILD'S-EYE VIEW
"Say Thank You"

No more doctors! Chloe squirms on her mommy's lap, wishing she could pry open the arms clamped around her and escape this tiny room. "Doctor Dan" has already poked Chloe's tummy with a stethoscope and stuck a flashlight in her ears. His strange behavior—kneading the area around her neck, peering into her eyes—has excited her curiosity and made her feel uncomfortable at the same time. But the worst is yet to come. A lady in a white lab coat enters, saying something about "hurting just a little." Chloe recognizes that white coat. *Not good!* She struggles, but before she knows what's happening, the lady jabs a needle into her arm. "Aaaaaaaaagh!" Chloe screams, but the needle is already gone and the woman is out the door.

"It's okay, Chloe," her mother says as she carries her out to the waiting room. But Chloe cries even harder. It most definitely is *not* okay! *Who was that lady? Why did Mommy let me get hurt?*

Next thing Chloe knows, she's sitting on the counter at the receptionist's desk. "Look!" her mother tells her. "Ms. Daley has a present for you!"

Sniffling, Chloe wipes her eyes and turns to look at the receptionist. She's smiling at Chloe—but she has a lab coat on, too! *Who's she?* Chloe wonders, panic rising again. *Is she going to hurt me, too?*

"Take the cookie, Chloe," Mommy says, squatting down beside her daughter and pointing to the cookie in Ms. Daley's hand. "Don't forget to say 'Thank you.' "

Is that lady good or bad? Chloe can't figure it out. But the cookie hovers tantalizingly near. Chloe looks back and forth between Mommy and the stranger with the cookie. "Sank you," she says uncertainly.

The strange woman's face lights up in a big smile. So does Mommy's. Mommy gives Chloe a kiss. "Good, Chloe," she says. "You're so polite."

As she leaves the office, Chloe chews the cookie meditatively. *One white coat hurt me,* she thinks. *One gave me a cookie. When you get a cookie, you say "Thank you." When you get hurt, you . . .* She shakes her head. The ways of adults just bewilder her sometimes. All she knows is, she was a "good girl." She said "Thank you." And the cookie tastes sweet.

"YOU BE THE BABY": GROWING SOCIALLY THROUGH PLAY

It would be easier, perhaps, if our children looked to us alone for information on how to express themselves socially, but one of the hallmarks of this third year is their increasing interest in other children. Your two-year-old may be quietly paging through a picture book in the library when a group of shrieking kids races into the room. Impressed, your child stops what he's doing and shrieks, too. Even if the newcomers race off and are never seen again, you may have to put up with your own child's shrieks in the library for weeks afterward, until you can persuade him that that particular form of social expression is a bad idea.

Of course, other children's influence can be a very positive force as well—a girl in the park may offer her trike to your child, modeling good behavior—and playing together allows children to practice the social rules that they've just begun to learn. Your two-year-old may not be able to sustain a friendly interaction with a child his age for more than a few minutes at a time, but during these brief episodes of mutual imitation (making a noise, responding to it, making it again), cooperation (building blocks together side by side), and pretend (talking to each other on toy phones), he will learn much about the rewards and requirements of social give-and-take. His experiences with slightly older children can prove even more stimulating as these "mentors" introduce him to more sophisticated activities such as games with rules (hide-and-seek), role-playing (teacher and student, doctor and patient), and scene enactment (conducting a tea party, escaping a monster). Since children are much more likely than adults to repeat such activities over and over, your child will be able to explore many more aspects of the game than he might if you were playing it with him.

In fact, one of the greatest forces for social growth may be living right in your home. Studies have shown that, while interacting with any child expands a two-year-old's social and cognitive awareness, playing with and observing *familiar* children has an even stronger influence on them. Not only is your child familiar with his siblings and already embroiled in a complex social relationship with them, but his brothers and sisters are frequently available for social interaction and can be observed communicating in a variety of ways with the parents. Rest assured, then, that your youngest is watching carefully—and even listening from the next room—as you talk with your other children. Whatever tactics they use to achieve their goals are bound to be imi-

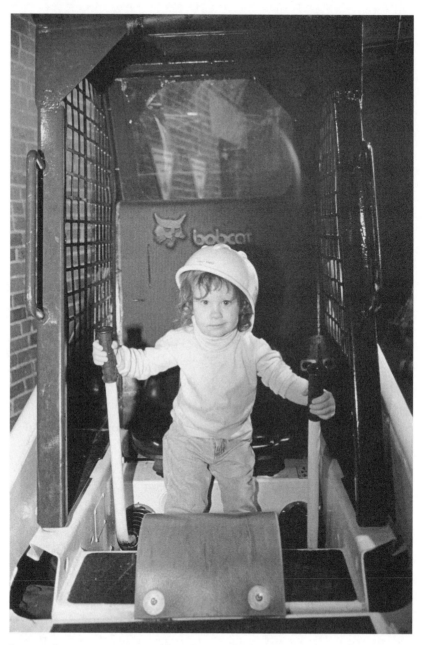

Surrounding your two-year-old with varied play experiences allows her to explore without preset limits.

tated. You can make the best of this situation by pointing out to your two-year-old his older sibling's appropriate behavior ("Look—David helped clean up his room this morning,") and refusing to reward rudeness or selfishness, particularly when your two-year-old is watching.

Part of learning about social interaction includes learning about gender roles and gender-related behavior. Your child's general interest in classifying objects (a cow is an animal, blue is a color) will naturally spur him to classify himself as a boy or girl. At first, though, he won't have more than a vague idea of what this classification means. He may think of a girl as someone with long hair—and so will assume that a male teenager with a ponytail is a girl. His idea of a boy as, say, a short-haired person wearing pants will be so strong that you could remove the dress from a female doll, put the doll in pants, and cut its hair right in front of him, and he would call it a boy. His concept of "boyness" and "girlness" will remain vague through the end of the year, and he'll probably make many mistakes in categorizing people.

In the same way, his gender-related *behavior* will waver quite a bit. His "boy-like" or "girl-like" preferences (play fights versus tea parties), if any, will remain vague and change constantly. If he is enrolled in preschool or some other group care program, he may feel the urge to imitate others who are "like" himself and thus indulge in more gender-typical play. Consciously or not, you and your child's other caregivers will also affect how gender-typed his play is at this age, as evidenced by a 1991 study by Beverly Fagot. She showed that parents most strongly direct their children's play according to gender at eighteen months, and other studies show that parents' gender-related attitudes and behavior continue to hold sway for years to come.

As this year progresses, your child's awareness of adult interactions increases, feeding his curiosity about what it means to be a boy or a man, a woman or a girl. He will note that Daddy behaves in one way and performs certain social tasks, while Mommy behaves in different ways—and these observations will spur him to think about which way *he* will act. At this point, he may begin to imitate his same-sex parent's social behavior—playing office like Dad and imitating his speech mannerisms or movements. Most parents unconsciously reinforce this kind of gender learning and even shut their young children down when they cross the gender line ("Donny is *not* dressing as Wonder Woman for Halloween!"). It's important to understand, however, that your child is only *observing* and *imitating* differences in behavior—he is not expressing any deeper urges. He certainly has no understanding that behaving like a member of the opposite sex *means* something to adults ("Is he gay?"), and his cross-gender experimentation is not necessarily an indication of his future tendencies.

If gender issues are important to you, or a source of contention between you and your partner, this is a good time for both of you to think about what your feelings and behavior are teaching your child. Any anxiety you feel about your child's gender-related behavior, or about the subject of gender in general, is far more likely to affect your child's attitudes than his actions themselves. (He will suffer from dressing up as Wonder Woman only if you or others he cares about react negatively.) It's better to keep things very simple this year—helping your child experiment with gender roles through imaginative play, keeping some nonstereotypical toys around to allow him to explore less familiar territory, and giving brief, nonjudgmental answers to his questions as a way of laying the groundwork for future discussions. Keep in mind that these issues will grow much stronger and more valid at age three and older.

Exploring and experimenting with gender roles, even at the level of a two-year-old, does give your child an exciting preview of what it's like to be an individual in the larger world. Though the persona he adopts today is no more likely to express his mature social "self" than the one he adopts tomorrow, it is a sign that he is thinking about social interaction in much more sophisticated and interesting ways. The more he is able to play with these concepts—to understand how he is like or unlike Mommy, how he resembles or does not resemble Dad, how both Mom and Dad are good at some things—the more self-confident he'll feel as he strides into the challenging world of preschool and other group activities. This confidence is very important as he interacts with and is judged by teachers, parents, and other adults who don't already know him.

Social development is not all about learning rules and studying gender roles, of course. Playing with others is fun, and we all hope our children will enjoy the pleasures of friendship. By his third year, your child interacts in much more complex and positive ways with others his age than he ever did before. He can distinguish between his playmates and even develop comfortable routines as he interacts with the partners he knows best. Though months or even years must pass before he begins to truly understand the difference between an acquaintance and a friend, the foundations for close peer relationships are being laid down this year. Slowly, day by day, he is learning to cooperate, to show affection, and to settle disagreements. He is beginning to consider the concept of fairness and to understand that his playmates have rights that may be as valid as his. As he celebrates his third birthday—surrounded, perhaps, by some of the children who've helped him explore these issues—he can surely look forward to years of rich, fulfilling, and ever-developing friendships.

Q & A
My Quiet Child

Q: My daughter, Hillary, has never seemed very interested in other kids. When I take her to any social event, she clings to my skirt and cries if I try to pry her off of me. I didn't used to let it bother me much, but now that she's nearly three, her behavior is beginning to seem unusual. I'd like to enroll her in preschool next year, but I'm worried that she won't be able to handle the social aspects of it. She doesn't have any brothers or sisters, and the play dates I've arranged have all been washouts, since she refuses to interact with her guests. Is her behavior normal? If not, what should I do?

A: Your child is apparently shy by nature (many, many young children are), but whether or not this is the case, she could probably benefit from learning some specific ways to relate to other children and practicing them in simple, nonthreatening contexts. Set the bar low at first—expose her to informal encounters with other children in places she already knows, such as the children's museum, the library, or the pond where you go to feed ducks. Model good social initiatives for your child (saying to another child, "Would you like to feed the ducks, too?"). Comment on the positive results ("Look—she smiled!"). Don't put pressure on your child to talk to the newcomer, but allow them to continue their activity together, side by side. With time, your child will begin to feel more comfortable and may even respond when the child makes a move toward her.

Once your daughter seems more comfortable just being with another child, arrange for a play date, preferably with a child she already knows reasonably well. Before the play date, act out parts of it with your daughter, suggesting play ideas ("Maybe Trish will want to play ball"). Discuss which toys she'd like to share with her visitor, and help her put the others away. Structure the play date so that your child doesn't feel she must shoulder the entire social burden herself. Plan to help the two of them bake muffins, play dress-up together, or volunteer to be "it" in a game of hide-and-seek. And talk about what she should do if the other child hits, refuses to share, or behaves in any other way that she fears. When the time for the play date arrives, read a magazine nearby or otherwise stay unobtrusively within sight, so you can be there to support her if she becomes uneasy. If you can help her enjoy one play date, she is more likely to look forward to another. In this way, little by little, you can help her curb her innate resistance and find ways to begin making friends.

"GO AWAY!": SOCIAL LABELING AND REJECTION

"I'll never forget the first time I met Hector," a client told me during a visit. "I guess every neighborhood just has to have a bully, and even at two and a half, Hector was ours. Even though he was the youngest kid on the block, he was big for his age and looked about three or four. The first time I saw him was at an outdoor barbecue, and he was pushing a child to the ground for the third time since he and his mother had arrived. You should have seen the looks on the other parents' faces as his mother dragged him away from that screaming four-year-old. It didn't matter that Hector was only two and didn't know how to act as old as he looked. It didn't matter that his mom was eight months pregnant and he was probably mad about the baby. Everyone at that barbecue had already labeled Hector a bully. He's five now, and he still has that reputation. I think he's given up trying to fight it."

Few social issues are more painful for many parents than the notion that their child may be negatively labeled by his peers. Memories of children's taunts ("Tattletale!" "Wimp!" "Crybaby!") still haunt many of us, and we may worry a great deal about our own kids suffering from them. Though two-year-olds are rarely in a position to be labeled or rejected, it is not too early to teach them how to avoid the social behavior that often leads to such treatment, as my client's story illustrates. If Hector's mother had monitored him more closely, considered his angry state, and *prevented* him from pushing other children rather than pulling him away afterward, she might have been able to shape his behavior in ways that would have improved his relations with the adults in his life as well as with other children.

Refraining from aggression is not the only social skill your child will need to gain acceptance among his peers. He will need to know how to express positive feelings and how to respond to his friends' positive gestures. He will have to know how to express his thoughts and interests in ways that will engage others' attention. He must be able to lead as well as follow. He should know how to have fun and how to share his enthusiasm with others. He must also learn how to control his negative feelings rather than letting them erupt too often in angry words or tears.

Many of these prosocial abilities develop naturally from your child's interaction with you and others in his immediate circle. Some may run contrary to his natural temperament, and he may need help and encouragement from you to develop them. If you feel, for example, that your very active two-year-old routinely overwhelms other children—either physically by knocking against them frequently or invading their personal space, or verbally by interrupting frequently and refusing to listen—now is the time to begin teaching him specific ways to leave room for others. If he is a sensitive child who cries easily, it makes sense to keep his interactions short, remain nearby to redirect him in difficult situations, and talk with him frequently about how you and others manage your own anxious feelings. In general, it is important to keep in mind that younger two-year-olds are not able to interact in positive ways in many kinds of situations. As I pointed out in the previous chapter, your best bet in starting your child on the road toward social acceptance is, whenever possible, to circumvent situations that you know he can't yet handle, to teach him the basic rules and tools of social interaction, and to support him in his efforts to control his own destructive impulses.

As your child nears age three and engages in more group activity, he is more likely to encounter gender-based exclusion, particularly from older children. At this age, it is quite startling and confusing to hear two or three girls shout, "Go away! No boys here!" or vice versa. Unpleasant as this kind of rejection is, it happens all the time among preschoolers (and older children as well). Some professionals believe that exclusion serves a valuable function, helping children preserve social groups that they've only just learned to form and enabling them to hang on to a stable identity. It may also protect their play from disruption by outsiders—particularly those who are likely to play differently.

Rather than condemn exclusionary behavior when your child reports it, consider using it as an opportunity to discuss (at a simple level) the entire issue of labeling and exclusion ("It's sad when you want to make new friends but the kids won't let you play"). Such a conversation may reveal fears or anxieties you didn't know he had. Teaching him specific, concrete ways to deal with such behavior will go much further in helping him manage his world than criticizing the other children or complaining to the adult in charge. You might also read one or more of the many children's books that deal with this issue on a level he can understand. Finally, casually acknowledging the existence of certain social dynamics ("Lots of times people in a group don't want newcomers to join in") lets your child know that he has not been rebuffed for personal reasons and that it is quite likely that on another day the group will accept him gladly.

EASING THE WAY
Crisis Management

It's easy enough for most of us to talk to our kids about playing fairly and being gentle with those who are smaller than us—but successfully managing an actual fight can be a greater challenge. On a typical day, every playground in every neighborhood resounds with cries of, "Get off me!" and, "Ow!" It's hard to know what to do—or how to restrain your own emotions—when you see your child hit or pushed by another child, or even ignored or insulted by adult. The best approach may be to look on these inevitable skirmishes as a learning experience. Since such demoralizing encounters are unfortunately part of every-one's life, you can best help your child by teaching him how to deal with them and move on.

When your child turns to you in tears after a child has hurt him, resist the impulse to, on the one hand, rationalize that child's behavior or, on the other, to label him as "bad" or a "bully." (Remember, next time the aggressor could be your child.) Acknowledge that the child "made a mistake" or "doesn't know the rules," and that "pushing was wrong."

Model an effective response by putting a hand on the other child's hand and saying, "Don't do that. It isn't nice. Let's do this instead." Then, as the child demonstrates better behavior, focus on the positive by saying, "Look, he's sharing now." Ideally, the parent of the other child will cooperate in this effort (and you should certainly enlist the aid of the other parent if you can). Whether or not other adults cooperate, however, your job this year is to demonstrate a positive response for your child so that he'll be able to deal with others' hurtful behavior in the future.

"WANT SOME?": PRACTICING CONSIDERATION

Part of joining the larger world is learning to empathize and show kindness to other people. Your child's developing awareness of the world around him this year will increase his ability to consider others' feelings and to want them to be happy. This is a different experience from his tendency as a toddler to look concerned when you were upset, or the vague but gentle pat he may have offered last year when he found you crying. Last year he could compare your sadness to similar feelings he had felt and be moved to comfort you. Now, his mind has developed to the point where he is actually able to see things from another person's point of view (particularly those who are closest to him), to think about what might make that person happy, and to act on his empathic impulses.

This doesn't mean that your two-year-old will regularly offer his toys to restless playmates or play quietly by himself when he realizes you need a rest. Though he may *understand* the state you're in to some extent, he still finds it very difficult to put aside his own needs to tend to yours or anyone else's. When encountering another person's distress, he can easily feel threatened, his fragile sense of self dissolving in the face of the other's tears. If he sees that Brandon is scared, he may won-

Sharing and taking responsibility are two prosocial tasks that you can begin to instill in your two-year-old.

der whether he should be, too. This uncertainty makes him more likely to cry, act aggressively, or leave the scene than to console Brandon or try to cheer him up. In other instances, he may simply not yet know what to do to ease another person's unhappiness (such as offering his company to a child playing alone). It is also true that two-year-olds are so accustomed to seeing adults help an unhappy child that they may hang back and wait for a grown-up to make things better.

Fortunately, your child will make another discovery this year that will help him act on his empathic impulses. He will begin to understand more clearly the concept of personal agency—things don't just happen but are *made* to happen. His baby sister stops crying, for example, when he gives her a pacifier. His growing familiarity with this idea may lead to a fascination with the concept of personal *responsibility.* Once this happens, many older two-year-olds quite suddenly transform into solemn commentators on each family member's misbehavior ("Mommy, Mikey didn't share."). Annoying as this habit can be to his siblings, you can at least assure them that he's not turning into a tattletale (he's not old enough for that). He's just suddenly interested in how right and wrong behavior occur. Reward his interest by affirming his intuition that Mikey did something wrong (out of Mikey's hearing, of course) and talking about the positive behavior that Mikey might have chosen instead.

Understanding that he and others can make things happen will soon lead your child to the idea that people can affect each other's emotional states as well. Now is the time for him to begin acting on his positive urges in this area. He will need plenty of instruction on precise ways to do so. Especially near the beginning of this year, simple, concrete instructions and explanations ("Don't take that cookie away from Henry. It will make him sad") work much better than confusing general comments ("Frank, remember to share!"), which he isn't yet equipped to comprehend. As he begins to understand what behavior is expected and act correctly, you can simply acknowledge the fact that he has done so ("Look how you shared with Henry. Good for you!"). As he reaches the end of this third year, it's a good idea to talk about such behaviors even when they're not actually happening and to discuss situations that are likely to arise ("Remember, when Henry gets here, you'll need to share your toys"). It's also important to articulate the reasons behind such behavior—to talk about how a child feels when a playmate shares with him, comforts him, and so on. As your child increasingly shows interest in his own and others' feelings, comment on them frequently yourself. When reading storybooks, discuss with him how the hero feels at a certain point in the story and why, and what the hero might do to make himself or another feel better. Help your child try to remember when he felt the same way. And don't forget to talk about your own feelings, too. It is an amazing, reassuring discovery for young children to realize that their parents experience sadness, excitement, hope, envy, discomfort, and doubt, just as they are beginning to feel these complex emotions themselves.

Age two is a time to begin these lessons, but it is not a time to expect perfection in carrying them out. As in all areas of growth, your child will need to experiment with many variations in behavior before settling down to those that work best for him. For this reason, you can expect him to expend a great deal of energy violating the very types of behavior you're trying to teach him. At some point, he'll probably enjoy challenging you in ways that run contrary to your expectations about relationships ("I don't love you, Mommy!"), honesty ("I didn't do it!"), or good behavior ("I won't share!"). Difficult as it is to put up with these experiments, it's important for you to provide the correct responses. By calmly reminding your child that *you* love *him,* that you know he didn't tell the truth, or that if he doesn't share his friend won't want to keep playing with him, you reassure him that the world is as it should be and that the standards he is learning really are important.

By his third birthday, your child's ability to tolerate delays and to restrain his immediate impulses will have improved a great deal. These two developments will go a long way toward helping him become a kinder, more thoughtful person. As he grows, he will get better at understanding others' points of view, cooperating, and thinking of ways to express his empathy. As a result, family life should improve markedly over the next few years, if not always at a smooth pace.

IF YOU'RE CONCERNED
Social Challenges

The third year is not an extremely social one for all children, and it is not fair to expect your child to enjoy playing with other children most, or even part, of the time. He has much work to do in understanding his own thoughts and emotions before he can focus fully on others his age. Children's social skills do not really develop until between ages two and a half and five. There's no point in expecting these abilities to manifest themselves before then. However, if your older two-year-old shows *no* interest in other children, or if his behavior causes others to avoid, taunt, or complain about him, now is certainly the time to observe his interactions carefully and consider the reasons behind them.

The amount of time your child spends playing with other children is not the only gauge of how well he's growing socially. If he plays often with others but almost always takes on the same role (the follower rather than the leader, for example) or plays in nonproductive ways (constantly teasing or otherwise provoking the other child), he may need more focused attention from you before he can begin to manage relationships more successfully. A child who frequently hovers at the edge of a group of children, hoping in vain to be invited to join in, or one who smiles eagerly at a peer but doesn't know how to engage him in play, could clearly use some instruction in how to get to know someone new. If your child seems to prefer swinging all afternoon, on the other hand, or is content to go up and down the slide by himself, he is probably just not focused on social issues right now and will pick up his "people skills" easily enough when his time comes. However, if he maintains a low level of play activity beyond his third birthday, try to pull him out of himself. Too much time spent alone may lessen the amount of stimulation he receives, limit his cognitive growth, and leave him stuck in behavioral patterns that don't work well for him. Make a point of engaging him in a social activity, and show him through modeling, talk, and encouragement the joys of playing with others.

"ME, AND YOU, TOO": THE BEGINNINGS OF FRIENDSHIP

It's Thursday, and nearly time for the biweekly play date that Eileen and Mary have arranged for their two sons for nearly a year. Noel, two weeks from his third birthday, can hardly wait for Jeff to appear at his front door. "Jeff is coming today!" he keeps cheerily reminding his mom. "Jeff is my friend!" Eileen is also looking forward to the play date, which is so easy to prepare for at this point. She has a good idea of what kinds of activities each boy will want to do. She knows which toys are likely to keep them playing happily, and which ones to hide upstairs before Jeff's arrival to prevent a fight or overly aggressive play. Once she and Mary realized that it was wiser to chat in the same room with their boys than off in the kitchen on their own, they quickly picked up on the directions in which each child's personality was evolving. Fortunately, the two boys' temperaments seem to complement each other—Jeff's generosity sometimes inspires Noel to share more readily, and Noel's enthusiasm for imaginary play leads Jeff into more complex thinking. The boys appear to sense that it's a good match, too, Eileen muses. There's a rhythm between them that allows for more fun and less conflict than earlier in the year.

Just as Eileen is pulling Noel's construction kit from the toy box, the doorbell rings. "Jeff's here!" Noel cries, running to the door. Eileen opens it and greets Mary as Jeff races past them to embrace her son. "*Finally* you got here!" Noel says with satisfaction, pulling Jeff by the hand into the living room. "I couldn't *wait* to play!" Mary and Eileen glance at each other, amused. It's really true, then, Eileen says to herself. Noel has made a friend.

Social Achievements in the Third Year

24 MONTHS   Imitates other children's behavior

Enjoys playing with older children

May begin to share

Sometimes empathizes with another's emotions

27 MONTHS   Siblings become more significant members of his social world

May enjoy play groups

30 MONTHS   Begins to comprehend the concept of a friend

Wants to be the center of attention

33 MONTHS   May benefit from group care or preschool

Starts taking control of play with peers

36 MONTHS   Is able to learn and remember social rules and customs

Becomes more interested in the concept of gender and gender-related behavior

FIRST-PERSON SINGULAR

It's a sad fact of life that many of us forget the names of those friends who meant so much to us when we were very young. Take a moment to record here the names of your child's first playmates. Describe the activities they enjoyed most together, and those that most often led to arguments. Don't forget to record the instances when your child acted kindly to someone else, decided to tell the truth in a difficult situation, or mastered his own impulses in favor of someone else's needs. Include your thoughts on the social preferences your child seems to be demonstrating—is he sociable or solitary, active or passive, a leader most of the time or a follower? It will be interesting to find out how many of these social traits last into adolescence and adulthood—and fascinating to realize how many don't!

READER'S NOTES

_____

_____

_____

_____

_____

_____

_____

_____

_____

_____

_____

_____

_____

_____

_____

_____

_____

_____

_____

CHAPTER 7

A Stable Platform—My Need
for Routine

Your two-year-old is a stickler for order and correctness—at least in others.

Thirty-three-month-old Annie's caregiver, Martha, has decided to move back to her distant hometown, and Annie's entire family is sad to think that Martha will no longer be a regular part of their lives. In the two years since Martha began caring for Annie full-time, she has become a friend and confidante to Annie's older sister, Rose, a dependable partner to parents Jane and Luke, and a trusted source of love and support for Annie herself. As much as Jane will miss Martha, she's comforted by the fact that she'll be between jobs when Martha leaves, and that she and Luke can care for her daughter full-time for a while. It should be relatively simple to take up the reins in Martha's absence, Jane reasons. As the time for the transition approaches, she looks forward with increasing excitement to spending more time with Annie.

At first, the transition seems to go reasonably well. Martha and Jane both carefully explain to Annie that Martha will soon move away to be closer to *her* mom. Martha gives Annie a picture of herself as a memento and promises to write as soon as she arrives at her new home.

Annie clearly doesn't understand most of what Martha is saying, but she responds to this talk of change much more calmly than Jane had expected. Jane's job ends a few days before Martha leaves. After a tearful good-bye to Martha, mother and daughter begin their full-time life together.

For the first few days, the novelty of her new home situation seems to keep Annie in a daze. She gives her mom puzzled glances and asks, "Where'd Martha go?" Her behavior makes Jane nervous—is Annie going to fall apart when she realizes Martha isn't coming back? To reassure her, Jane takes her on a special field trip each day for the first week. They visit the local aquarium. They visit the children's museum. They join another two-year-old and her mom at the beach for the day. The harder Jane works to distract Annie, however, the more the little girl seems to crumple. By the end of the week, she has practically stopped talking—shrieking instead when she doesn't get her way, and crying for no reason at all. Her recent progress in toilet training has disintegrated, too. She wets her pants three times over the weekend. And every time an adult asks her to do something, she refuses with a pout and a resounding "No!"

"I just wish I knew what she's thinking," an exhausted Jane confesses to her husband Sunday night. "I mean, I know she misses Martha. But this seems like it's about even more than missing someone. She just can't seem to get her bearings."

In fact, Annie *is* having trouble adjusting to the changes in her life—not only the change in caregivers but the sudden disruptions in the routines embedded in her day-to-day life. Two-year-olds rely heavily on patterns they can predict—repeated sequences that allow them to believe they can comprehend their environment, thus bolstering their self-confidence. When Annie's lifelong caregiver abruptly disappears *and* her recently mastered routines of breakfast-while-Mommy-gets-dressed-for-work, bye-to-Mom-and-Dad-hi-to-Martha, coloring-with-Martha-after-breakfast, are disrupted, she feels as though all her supports have been removed at once. Her mother's well-meaning attempts to distract her from Martha's absence have in fact increased

Annie's discomfort as she struggles to find something in her world that *hasn't* changed.

Even if your family has experienced no major disruptions this year (a new baby in the family, a new home, a divorce or remarriage), you will find that your two-year-old is a stickler for order and correctness—at least in other people. Determined to live in a world she can master and control, she can be counted on to make sure you stick to your routines ("Bedtime story!") and to experiment with challenging them ("No bath!"). Much of the time, her determined preoccupation with protocol may amuse you ("Kiss on the nose first, *then* on the chin!"). Sometimes it will seem more maddening than cute ("No pink pants! Blue!"). In nearly every case, however, your child behaves as she does because she has little choice—routines are her lifeboat, her major source of security in a world that's still often confusing. They're the platform from which she can launch herself toward further exploration.

Because routines are so important to your child, it makes sense to pay attention to the ones you and your child develop together this year. Ideally, they will be healthy practices that you're willing to live with for one, two, or more years to come. They should suit your child's energy level and temperament, leave some room for variety so that your child is regularly stimulated, but also come with a clear bottom line that is never violated. And they should be carried out with reasonable predictability by the other caregivers in your child's life. A regular half-hour of children's television after lunch might provide a pleasant rest, for example, for a two-year-old who is transitioning out of naptime—as long as the child is not so active that she has a hard time sitting still. Each day's changing theme provides a subject for discussion between the two of you, and your refusal to give in to her repeated demands for more TV shows her that this is a routine she can rely on. On days when someone else gives her lunch, the expected half-hour of television or videotape reassures her that life is predictable even in your absence. She begins to think of this as "her" TV time, as pleasing and satisfying as a favorite possession—and her parents enjoy the mental health break, too.

As her language and cognitive skills improve this year, establishing routines becomes easier in some respects. Your child will begin to comprehend, at least partially and at least for the moment, the *reasons* you give her for completing certain actions (a bath will clean off germs and relax her before bedtime) and the *results* of violating them (toys left on the floor can get stepped on and broken). She can also begin to contribute her own ideas about how to alter or create some routines, adding to their richness and utility. By asking her opinion on whether a night-light or an open bedroom door might best help her go to sleep at night, you demonstrate a respect for your child's needs and encourage her to start thinking of ways to structure her own daily life. It is also important to remember, however, that giving your child *too much* choice in routine matters (letting her decide what she wants to wear each day, asking whether she wants the crust cut off the sandwich bread) may lead to endless negotiating and resistance that you will regret in later years. In looking for a happy medium, focus on making it clear that you're the parent, and though your child is invited to contribute her input, you still have the final word.

Of course, predictable routines will not make all parenting problems go away this year, even if your child does help create them. Mealtimes will continue to challenge both of you if she continually refuses food and you worry about time wasted, messes made, and calories left unconsumed. Toilet training, a major routine-related issue for many families this year, is nearly always accompanied by regressions, misunderstandings, and lapses in patience on both your parts. Important routines that have no clear, immediate benefit for your child—such as cleaning up after playtime, brushing her teeth twice a day, or putting on her snowsuit before she plays outside and then taking it off when she comes back in—will be hard to implement at this age when she is still unable to think in long-term or general terms. Nevertheless, your child will look to you this year to decide which routines are important and to explain (again and again) exactly why. By meeting her need for a certain level of predictability, you will help her begin to comprehend a great deal more about why we humans live as we do, what is (or should be) important to us, and how we can move through our days productively.

Q & A
Predictability Rules

Q: Our thirty-month-old son, Kenny, is a creature of extreme habit. He hates to do anything differently than he's done it before—to the extent that we can hardly ever get him to try anything new. He refuses to try swinging on the big kids' swings on the playground because he's always swung on the infant swings. He screams his head off if he can't find his stuffed bunny at bedtime. And he absolutely will not eat anything besides the few foods he liked when he was one. It gets really tiresome trying to introduce him to new experiences when he resists them so much. How can we open him up to a little variety and change?

A: How much or how little a two-year-old is willing to leap into new experiences depends in large part on the child's temperament, as well as on his phase of development. Parents may have an effect as well, by throwing too many new experiences at a child who can't handle them or overly limiting a more active child's environment. Your two-year-old apparently leans toward the less adventurous end of the temperamental range for this age, but rest assured that nearly all parents of two-year-olds meet much more resistance to novelty than they expect. Saying no to new input—and even more challenging, suggesting their own alternative—is a relatively new skill for a thirty-month-old. Refusing or countering your offers can be a heady experience. Sticking to what he knows also gives him a necessary feeling of control and gradually increases his self-confidence.

To get a more objective feel for whether your child's resistance is abnormal, look around at other kids his age to see whether they're equally stubborn. Consider whether you're troubled about this issue because it clashes with your own temperament or because it's truly a cause for concern. Ask other parents who know your child, or have had experience with a similar child, for their opinions and suggestions. Then, if you still feel your child has a problem, talk about this issue with his pediatrician at his next checkup. Keep in mind that most two-year-olds begin to grow a little less rigid during the second half of this year. By age three, if he hasn't been pushed too hard to experiment beyond his comfort level, he should begin to feel somewhat more secure about things as they are and become more open to experiencing something different. He'll probably still rely on routines as he grows older, but the influence of friends and other acquaintances should increase his flexibility.

"LEAVE THE LIGHT ON": SLEEP PATTERNS IN THE THIRD YEAR

"I always felt so lucky when other parents complained about their kids' sleep habits," Andrea, a mom I met on the playground, confessed to me recently. "I don't know why, but my son, Eugene, settled into a great sleep routine at about nine months of age and never really fell out of it until he was two. Then, when I decided he was ready to start skipping his afternoon nap, everything fell apart. I couldn't get him up in the mornings, so then he wouldn't go to sleep till late that night, he'd sleep late again the next day, and the whole time he acted tired and cranky. I tried having him take a nap again, but he couldn't settle down. It took me half the year to work things out with him."

Andrea didn't know it at the time, but her experience with Eugene was actually quite common. By the time your child is two, you have no doubt created some kind of bedtime routine with her—whether it consists of a bath, a story, and her security blanket at eight-thirty or falling into your bed together, exhausted, at ten or eleven. Whatever the routine, she's grown accustomed to it, and even as she resists the nightly ritual, she has begun to understand that there's no avoiding it. At around this time, however, a number of elements come into play that can affect her reliance on (or resignation toward) her usual routine. Her verbal growth may leave her so mentally stimulated at the end of the day that she finds it hard to stop talking and settle down. Once alone, she is now able, owing to recent cognitive developments, to imagine spooky creatures in the darkness and even to experience a nightmare or two. Her improved physical skills enable her to climb out of her crib, if she's still sleeping in one, or to come to your room at night if she sleeps in a bed. Finally, the tendency of all young children to test and retest their parents' resolve will come into play again at bedtime this year.

As always when developing or changing routines with your child, it's best to tailor her bedtime ritual to her particular temperamental style, developmental stage, and home situation. If your child is a night owl and you want to start moving her toward an earlier bedtime, you may need to initiate some kind of physical activity in the evenings, such as a walk around the block or a mock-wrestling session, to help her adjust to the new schedule. If she is in a particularly resistant phase of development, encourage her to create some of her own rules for bedtime (one story plus an "extra," or three kisses from Mom plus a story on tape) so that she feels she's in control even as she falls asleep. If she shares a room with one or more siblings, it might be a good idea to put her to bed an hour before the others so that she'll be fast asleep by the time they enter the room. It is much more effective to observe the results of these experiments and change the routine in positive ways to suit your child than to adhere to the cookie-cutter bedtime rules laid out in many parenting articles and books.

Naptime is a particularly effective tool to use this year when adjusting your child's sleep schedule to better fit her own and the entire family's needs. Your child probably doesn't need to sleep as much during the day anymore, but a nap might help regulate a schedule that's gone awry. A non-napping child who's just started coming home from group child care at noon, for example, may be so tired that she frequently falls asleep around 5:00 P.M., wakes up an hour later, and finds it impossible to go to bed again until nearly midnight. If this child is encouraged to take an early nap right after coming home, she may adjust to her new schedule more easily. Even when you feel that any daytime sleep keeps your child up too late at night, it's still useful to build a regular rest period into her daily schedule. A brief rest can help your child learn how to create quiet time for herself, and it can regulate disrupted sleep schedules much as naps do. Andrea, for instance, might have reinstated a rest period for Eugene at least until he adjusted to a schedule without naps, to avoid having him swing unpredictably between a high-energy state and exhaustion.

For a number of reasons, sleep routines tend to grow easier as the third year progresses. Your child becomes able to work through her uneasiness about bedtime through conversations with you, imaginary play, an ability to narrate a book to herself or talk herself back to sleep, and greater understanding that you'll come back to her room in the morning. Outside routines may also make bedtime easier. Waking early to attend group care or preschool will make your child quite tired by the time dinner is over, and she will be more likely to fall asleep easily. (It's not a bad idea to wake her up at the same time on days when she does not have school, to keep her system on schedule.) Your own schedule may have become more predictable now that your toddler's life is more regulated, making it easier for both of you to stick to predictable routines. By your child's third birthday, you will at least have learned a great deal more about what helps your child get to bed on time, even if she still strenuously resists bedtime or has a hard time falling asleep. As you continue to build on those reliable aids—keeping the stuffed bunny on her pillow, for instance, while changing her waking-up and going-to-bed hours—the two of you should eventually be able to create a routine that works well enough for everyone.

A PARENT'S STORY
Jack's Room

"My son, Jack, slept in our room with us until he was two and a half," a neighbor told me recently. "He loved to snuggle with us and didn't really like sleeping in the crib next to our bed even when he was a baby, so I was worried about how I was ever going to get him out of there. Finally, my husband and I had had enough of sharing our space. We moved our two older boys into the same bedroom and gave the empty one to Jack.

"As it turned out, two and a half was the perfect time to make the change. Jack was at the height of his 'do-it-myself!' phase, and he really got into helping decorate his very own 'big-boy' room. He couldn't get over how cool it was to have his own real bed, like his big brothers', instead of a crib. He got to decide which stuffed animals got to stay on the bed and which had to go up on the top bookshelf. I let him pick out his own bedside lamp at the hardware store, and we made sure it had different settings so he could leave the light on low without admitting to his brothers that he was scared of the dark.

"Of course, the transition didn't happen all at once. For about six months or more after that, I spent plenty of nights keeping him company in his room till he fell asleep, and he would wake up in the middle of the night and come to our room at least two or three times a week. But we kept emphasizing how great it was that he had his own room now, and we let him control his own activities in there—letting him move around and look at books, as long as he stayed in bed. Over the long run, it really worked. Bedtime became a positive process instead of something painful that he had to force himself to go through."

"I *HATE* IT!":
NEW EATING ROUTINES

Feeding issues are often a major concern throughout the first three years of a child's life as parents move from breast-feeding or bottled-formula issues to introducing solids to trying to ensure a balanced diet in their child's daily life. The good news is that this is the year when many feeding challenges can finally be resolved. You will learn more about your

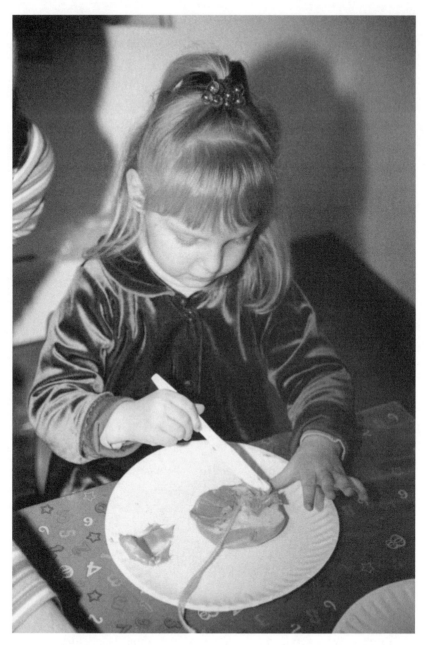

One way to reduce the inevitable feeding battles this year is to encourage your two-year-old to take control of some eating-related routines.

two-year-old's responses to various eating routines, and she will become more interested in eating as a social activity. The bad news is that children who were picky eaters as one-year-olds will probably continue to be so, especially during the first half of the year, when their resistant behavior may even make matters worse.

It helps to keep in mind, when trying to ensure that your child's eating routines lay the groundwork for proper nutrition, that two-year-olds don't need to consume as much food as parents sometimes assume. The American Academy of Pediatrics recommends that children between ages one and three consume about forty calories per inch of height a day. If your child is thirty-four inches tall, she should eat enough food to provide 1,350 to 1,400 calories per day. These amounts vary somewhat according to your child's metabolism, build, and level of activity, and she may eat a great deal one day and practically nothing the next. Fortunately, studies have shown that young children display a natural tendency to consume the correct number of calories over the course of a week if a range of foods is provided for them. Your job as parent is to make sure that the foods containing those calories are healthy ones—fruits and juice, vegetables, dairy products, whole grains, and meats or other proteins rather than (or at least much more than) soda, chips, sweets, and other non-nourishing treats. Of course, you don't have to offer a fresh-cooked meal three times a day, but do try to resist giving in to the ever-tempting convenience factor. Bad eating habits can be very hard to break.

As your two-year-old moves out of her high chair and takes a place at the family table, feeding issues may become more prominent and divisive than before. In particular, you and your partner may find yourselves embroiled in the "eat-everything-on-your-plate" versus "whatever-you-want-is-fine" debate. It is certainly true that frequent pressure on your child to eat what she doesn't want will most likely lead to stubborn refusal and even tears—and can even have a negative impact on her eating habits in years to come. On the other hand, preparing special meals just for her or allowing her to leave and return to the dinner table throughout the meal doesn't provide the structure she needs to learn to feed herself well. The most effective eating routines at this age seem to occupy the middle ground: cooking one meal for the entire family (but not making your two-year-old taste every dish); insisting that she stay at the table until she's finished eating (but not forcing her to stay until everyone else is done); encouraging her to try a new food by reminding her that she doesn't have to eat more than a bite if she doesn't like it; letting her help prepare the food she eats; letting her control what she puts *on* her food (parmesan cheese, butter, and so on); and refraining from criticizing or commenting on how much she has or hasn't eaten. This is a very difficult process for parents (and especially grandparents) who worry that the tiny amounts of food their children take in can't possibly sustain them. But the fact is that children never starve themselves as long as food is made available to them. When your child is hungry enough, she will stop demanding cold cereal and try a bowlful of spaghetti with tomato sauce instead.

Your child continues to be physically active this year, and there's nothing wrong with dropping a small snack into that little hand as she races by. Healthy finger foods such as bread, bagels, banana chunks, cooked carrot, cooked chicken, and cereal can go a long way toward providing the calories your child needs without forcing her to sit down and put her exciting life on hold. A wide and frequently changing variety of foods may also encourage her to eat more and try new foods. As you expand her diet, however, take care not to give her too much of a new food before you assess its effect. Two to 5 percent of children under age three suffer from food allergies, resulting in a range of reactions from skin rashes, diarrhea, watery eyes, sneezing, or a swollen throat to spasms or difficulty breathing. Pediatricians agree that most children outgrow the majority of these allergies by around age three, but it's important for her health as well as her enthusiasm for eating that you monitor her food intake until then.

As your child moves through the second half of this year, her increasing interest in social interaction may motivate her to spend more time at the dinner table, trying to participate in the family conversation. At this age, she will no doubt enjoy learning, practicing, and monitoring others' table manners (though she may start to resist if you put too much pressure on her to conform). Her skills won't be perfect by any means—she'll frequently use her hands instead of her spoon, wipe her face with her sleeve instead of her napkin, and knock over her "big-girl" cup of milk—but her inclusion in the group will mean a great deal to her, and she will work hard to earn her position. As she listens to her siblings describe a new video game between bites of the yucky food she refused a month ago, she may grow more curious about what everyone else is eating. Gradually, her resistance to newness may fade in the face of this new communal experience, and your child will learn to actually eat her food "like a big girl," too.

A CHILD'S-EYE VIEW
Broccoli Again

Mommy has just finished cooking dinner, and the house is filled with wonderful smells. Almost-three-year-old Rachel and her big brother, Gary, have finished setting the table (Rachel's job is to lay out the five napkins), and now everyone is taking a seat. *Meat,* Rachel says to herself eagerly as her dad lifts her into her toddler's chair. A big roast sits in the center of the table. Rachel breathes deeply, hardly able to wait till her mom slices a piece off and cuts it up on her plate.

"So how was work today?" Rachel, her eyes fixed on the meat now being cut up for her, is only vaguely aware of her parents' conversation. As soon as the knife pulls away, she grabs a piece and stuffs it into her mouth. *Mmmmm. Yummy.* She savors the juices, the texture of the beef, as Daddy's voice drifts toward her from the next chair: "Rachel, use your fork next time, okay?"

It takes a while for Rachel's hunger to abate, but after half a dozen more pieces of meat (two eaten with her hands, the rest with a fork, with Daddy's help), she feels relaxed enough to look around the table. Gary is talking about a chicken crossing a road. It's a joke—she can tell by his big, silly gestures and the way the others are smiling at him. Suddenly everyone erupts with laughter. Rachel is so preoccupied that she hardly notices her mother adding broccoli and mashed potatoes to her plate.

"I know a joke!" she shouts, bouncing in her chair and waving her arms around. To her great satisfaction, everyone now looks at her. "Okay," her brother Mike says. "What is it?"

For an instant, Rachel experiences only blankness where a joke should be. Then she remembers a phrase from a book her preschool teacher often reads. "Why'd the chicken cross the street?" she demands.

"Why?" asks Dad, smiling.

"Uh . . ." Rachel thinks for a long, painful moment. Then, spotting the first object in front of her, she says, "Because it was pepper!" To her relief, everyone laughs.

"Now I'll tell a joke," Mommy says. "But everybody take a bite first."

Jokes are fun. Rachel, beaming back at her family members, picks up a piece of food without looking and pops it into her mouth. *Yuck! Broccoli!* She starts to take it out. But then she hesitates. *Oh,* she thinks. *Butter. This is good.* Rachel chews thoughtfully, looking around the table as the conversation continues. She likes it here. She talks like the others, and she eats like them. She is a part of this family.

"I NEED GO POTTY": TOILET TRAINING

Few changes in routine are anticipated with more excitement and dread than toilet training as parents look forward to discarding expensive diapers and worry about pushing their children too hard. Certainly toilet training is one of the more difficult routines to establish, since there is no biological reason for a child to use a toilet rather than a diaper, and all her motivation must come from her environment. Nevertheless, parents of two-year-olds have a better chance of success than they would have had the year before. By age two, children are at least physically able to control elimination voluntarily—and the two-year-old's need to be a "big kid," with all the paraphernalia (including underwear and a potty or child's toilet seat), is a powerful motivating force. Near the beginning of the year, your child's preoccupation with the concept "mine" opens the way for you to present her with her very own personal potty. You might even give it to her as a birthday present and let her climb in it, turn it upside down, tote it from room to room, and otherwise claim it as her own. Her urge to imitate other children may motivate her to use the potty just to be like her older siblings or the girl across the street. Her love of order may increase her interest in learning where her body waste should go.

For these reasons, toilet training is probably *possible* this year, but it certainly isn't *necessary*. Don't be surprised if your two-year-old's periodic contrariness and sporadic attention get in the way of success. In general, it's best to keep the process positive (making the potty chair an attractive object, but not treating diapers or pull-ups as something for "babies") and not to push too hard or expect too much at this age. If you find that your child has lost interest or is actively resisting your efforts to get her out of diapers, drop the subject for now and wait for the next emotional and cognitive "window of opportunity." (Remember that toilet training is much more important to you than it is to her.) Times of major change—pregnancy, a move to a new house, a marital crisis—are certainly not the time to begin training. Even without such a major event, there's no real need to begin toilet training before age two and a half or three, unless she's required to be toilet-trained before entering a group program you have planned for her.

As with all aspects of your child's growth, you can most easily encourage her development by observing what her interests are at a given time. If she's becoming interested in the fact that you or her siblings use the potty, she'll show you in several ways: by choosing a book about potty use for her bedtime story, by hiding behind the couch when it's time to poop, or, like the little girl Denise in Chapter 1, by acting excited about the idea of wearing underwear. Once you've begun to note some of these signs, build on her interest by showing her a picture of a potty (and when you're ready, buying one for her) and talking about how all children learn to use one eventually. Let her spend time with you in the bathroom, just hanging out as you get dressed for the day. Let her watch you using the toilet—and if possible, other children using the potty—and buy some pull-ups or underwear for her to use when she's ready. Chances are good that your child will be eager to learn more about this mysterious process and will go along with your suggestion to sit on the potty with a book or toy once a day, even if she doesn't actually use it yet. Boys should be encouraged to sit on the potty, too, at first, so that they'll be in position when it's time to defecate. Later, when they begin to use the toilet more reliably, they can switch to a standing position—preferably with Dad's example and guidance.

Once your child is familiar with the general idea of a potty, it's time to prepare her to use it. First, she must make the connection between needing to eliminate and going to the potty. To help her do this, begin emptying her dirty diapers into the potty, explaining that this is where the poop goes. Once she's comfortable with this idea, start watching for moments when you see that she's about to have a bowel movement and offer to place her on the potty ("You look like you might want to go poop. Why don't we go find the potty?"). She may refuse, but at least the link between elimination and the potty will have been reinforced. (During this period, it's a good idea to let her wear underwear around the house—or nothing at all—so that you can get her to the potty quickly and easily once she does consent.) It will probably not be long before you manage to get your child into proper position at the right time. When she sees that she has actually accomplished the action you and she have been talking about, she will feel very proud.

It's important to praise this first accomplishment, but don't overdo it. You don't want your child to feel as though she's failed when she has an accident. Proudly inform the rest of the family about it, and make sure they praise her, too. This positive attention will convince your child that she is moving forward into the world of "big people" and motivate her to improve her skills even more. Don't expect her to follow up on her success right away. She needs time to process what has happened. In the meantime, praise *every effort,* follow her lead on diapers-versus-underwear and diapers-versus-potty, continue to put her on the potty just to sit once a day, offer her the potty when she's about to have a bowel movement, and talk about the issue in positive ways.

Gradually, her desire to imitate others and be a big girl will have its effect, and she will follow up more and more on her understanding that the potty is where she should eliminate. The two-year-old's love of step-by-step processes—pulling down her pants, sitting, getting toilet paper—should also motivate her. However, it's important to realize that there will be *many* exceptions, now and in the months and even years to come. Your child will probably wet her pants when she is upset, when she is too preoccupied with an activity to leave it, or when she is in an unfamiliar place. Her ability to wait to urinate is still quite minimal, and you will have to get her to a bathroom quickly once she announces that she needs to go. Be aware that some children feel uncomfortable, and therefore have difficulty, using an adult toilet, particularly away from home—so much so that they "hold it in" for an unhealthy length of time. Furthermore, young children who are already fully toilet-trained during the day may have trouble staying dry at night for quite a while. In fact, nearly half of all children in this country still wet the bed at age three. Most child development experts consider occasional bed-wetting normal until about six.

These accidents can be frustrating to a parent who believes that the toilet-training process is completed—and, of course, embarrassing when they happen in public. The adult often experiences such an incident as a failure on his or her own part, or as stubbornness or lack of cooperation on the child's part. It is vital to keep in mind, even when your child has urinated on the floor for the third time that day, that she is not doing it on purpose. Responding negatively, punishing her, or otherwise criticizing her efforts may well undo all your hard work up to this point and even make it necessary to start the training process over again. (If she gets a sufficiently emotional reaction from you by having an accident, she may just do it again soon to see whether you react the same way.) Instead, respond as you wish another adult would respond to you when you break a glass or accidentally cause some other kind of damage: sympathize with her, downplay the situation, and suggest a positive solution ("Oh, well, you'll get to the potty next time. Let's get some fresh underwear from your room"). Take a change of clothes along with you whenever you go out, to ease your own tension as well as her discomfort when something goes wrong. If her accidents continue occurring frequently, you might suggest pull-ups or even diapers again. Keep in mind that as long as you and her other caregivers are patient and maintain the routine for using the potty, she will conform to it when she's truly ready. By her third birthday, her desire to be a big girl and more frequent opportunities to observe other children her age who are toilet-trained (particularly in preschool and group care) will have given her another push to complete the process. And if she continues to resist, remind yourself that it is her body, after all, and that there's still plenty of time.

IF YOU'RE CONCERNED
Regression

Toilet training is a very uneven process, with many leaps forward and nearly as many leaps back. Most children move back and forth between the potty and diapers a number of times before settling on potty use most of the time. For some reason, boys tend to take longer to reach this settling point than girls do. Even twins sometimes pick widely different times to adjust to a potty or toilet, despite equivalent treatment. Overall, the toilet-training process may take several months to complete— not the couple of weeks that parents frequently expect when starting out.

Nevertheless, some children who are truly trained suddenly seem to forget their elimination routine over the course of a day or two and remain stuck in a regressive stage for a perplexingly long period of time. Usually, this regression is caused by an event that has distracted the child and occupied a great deal of her energy. A move to a new house, a change in caregivers, extended travel, or even a struggle to adjust to other changes in her life, such as a new sleep schedule or a big-kid bed, can cause your child to revert to diapers just when you were looking forward to moving on to other issues.

Such regression can be a minor problem for you, as you resign yourself to more cleanups and diaper purchases, but it need not be a major failure for your child if you have avoided treating accidents as a negative experience and telling her that diapers are "for babies." Simply offer her the pull-ups or diapers, wait for the distracting event to pass (or for your child to grow accustomed to it), and then begin training again. Reassure her that she "did it before and can do it again," stick to forward-thinking language ("Next time" and "Pretty soon"), keep her actively involved in the process (letting her pick the stall in the public bathroom, and letting her wash her own hands), and she will soon let you know that she's interested in trying again.

"WHERE AM I?": PLANNING AHEAD FOR TRAVEL

Many parents recall with dismay their attempts to travel with their one-year-old child. The one-year-old's desperate urge to keep moving, the ease with which she became disoriented and confused, and her short memory and attention span combined to make it a very difficult year to go for a long drive, much less get on a plane and visit someone cross-country. Fortunately, matters improve somewhat this year. Two-year-olds' longer attention span and greater ability to sit still make long periods in a car seat or airplane seat more bearable. The travel experience itself becomes more rewarding as young children's interest in other people and their surroundings increases. Still, two-year-olds' love of routine and occasional fearfulness or anger when their routines are disrupted can create new challenges.

When planning a trip, it helps to consider the prospect from your child's point of view. With only a tentative hold, if any, on new eating, sleeping, and elimination routines, she may feel her world slipping out of her control when the food she likes to eat is unavailable when she expects it, when she must fall asleep in a car seat instead of in her crib at home, or when she must try to use the bathroom on a noisy, uncomfortable airplane toilet. Many children respond to this challenge by either tightening up on routines (*insisting* on their usual foods, bedtime comfort objects, or potty) or abandoning them altogether and regressing. Since neither solution is ideal, it's best to try to keep your child's daily routines as close to normal as you can possibly make them. Pack her favorite foods for the trip, and try to give them to her at the usual times. Bring her favorite books or audiotapes along for the car, plane, or train ride. An activity book is an ideal way for a two-year-old to enjoy a regularly scheduled play period while remaining buckled into her seat. A simple pad and pencil, with which you can play tic-tac-toe and draw, can keep her calm for long stretches at a time. Once you're settled someplace for the night, be sure to produce her favorite stuffed animal and any other comfort object she needs to fall asleep. You might even pack a couple of familiar bath toys to help her through the trip.

One advantage your child has this year is her new verbal ability. You can use this skill to prepare her for the trip she's about to take and to interpret events for her as they happen. Talk to her about the trip and your destination, and show her pictures. Read a book about airports to her. She may not understand exactly what it means, but if you take the book along, you can point out a few bits of information when you arrive at the airport and refer to the book once you've boarded the plane.

The more you can prepare your child for any surprises or sudden changes, the more relaxed she'll feel about the travel process. Remember that even child-appropriate sights, such as a costumed character at a theme park, can frighten a young child who hasn't been told to expect it. Keep your senses attuned to unfamiliar sounds (an airplane's engine as it takes off), smells (the bathroom at a highway rest stop), textures (the stiff sheets at a hotel), sights (a camel at the zoo), and tastes (the bread in a foreign country) that are likely to set off her fear of the unknown, and comment on them in a calm, informative, even positive way.

In short, your child is capable of enjoying some vacation travel this year—but probably not much, and probably not often. The more calm and methodical you are about the process, the more likely she will be to let go of her fears and go along with your new, temporary travel routines. In the meantime, however, don't be surprised if she doesn't leap right into the exciting new experience you've planned for her this year. It doesn't mean she's unadventurous. It only means she's two.

EASING THE WAY
A Child's Itinerary

Many parents look forward to the day when they can take their children out into the world, introducing them to all its wonders. Two is an early age to begin this process, obviously, but there are ways to enhance your child's cognitive, emotional, and social growth through travel. The first rule to keep in mind is that your two-year-old retains much more information than is evident through her words or behavior. If you read her a children's book about camping in the mountains several times before leaving on your own trip, for example, she may not start spouting the names of different birds, but she *will* experience the trip much more fully than she would have otherwise. Not only will she be better prepared to enjoy the new sights, but she'll make countless interesting and stimulating connections between the characters and information in the book and what she sees in the actual place. By exposing her to this kind of experience, you're establishing a learning routine that can act as a valuable stepping-stone toward more active learning later on.

Emotional growth can be enhanced as your child learns that familiar routines are transferable to unfamiliar places. When *you* travel, do you like to take one or two familiar objects along with you, pack the same pajamas for each trip, or sleep on your usual side of the bed? Your child will experience the same reassurance these practices provide for you, but much more intensely. Be sure, then, not only that she brings a couple of comforting objects along, but that she participates in some of the same everyday activities—going for an evening walk, riding bikes, picnicking—that the family likes to do at home.

Social growth can be encouraged by making it easy for your child to interact with others. Traveling by train rather than plane allows her to walk with you from car to car, chatting occasionally with other passengers. If you fly, waiting to board allows your child to work out her energy in the airport, improving her chances of social success on the plane. A leisurely travel schedule leaves her with the energy and opportunity to meet people along the way.

By planning ahead, you can teach your child that traveling is a positive experience. Perhaps next year, she'll actually look forward to the family vacation.

"I HELPED!": SHARING AND COMPLETING TASKS

Two-year-olds long to be older, more powerful, and more in control of their day-to-day lives than they are. As they move toward age three, they are increasingly eager to take their place in the world, acting and being treated as equals in their family. Simple daily chores, far from being an imposition on them, allow them to "do it themselves"—to

Your child's desire to help can be encouraged by welcoming her involvement in daily tasks.

contribute to the family's well-being and thereby win the status they crave. Such chores should be real ones that provide assistance in a concrete way that the child can understand, and simple enough to allow her to complete them successfully. Laying out the place mats and napkins for dinner or holding the dustpan for you while you sweep up the dust lets your child experience tasks on a visceral, concrete level. When you or other family members comment on how well the job was done, your child swells with pride and her self-confidence increases.

It isn't necessary at this age for your child to have many tasks. Limiting her to a single duty each day is fine, as long as she is able to accomplish it herself from start to finish. Finishing the task for her defeats the purpose and may even teach her that there's really no need to finish things in the future. When initiating tasks, start small and simple. You might begin by asking your twenty-four-month-old to help you carry the laundry basket to the laundry room when you're ready to wash the clothes, thanking her profusely as she does so and commenting on how heavy the basket is. When she's a little older, you can assign her a two-part job, such as fetching the mail and then throwing away the empty envelopes as you go through it. Finally, you can let your child help decide which task she'll take on next. Let her choose from two tasks, and then be patient as she learns to do them well. Remember, this process is not about the task. It's about learning to cooperate, follow instructions, and stick to a commitment. It's about being part of the family.

Your two-year-old will benefit even more from completing tasks if they are a part of a routine that continues through the week. When she is expected to accomplish her chores each day, even when doing so isn't very convenient for parent and child, your child enjoys the satisfaction of knowing what to expect and of participating fully in family life. To help her mark her progress, create a chart listing each of her duties and let her attach a sticker for each task completed. You need not include only typical duties such as bringing the dog's food bowl to the kitchen to be filled or wiping off the table after dinner—you can add the personal tasks she's learning to accomplish such as using the potty or brushing her teeth. Don't forget to maintain such routines during play periods as well—insisting that toys be picked up (at least a little) and the caps replaced on markers before your child moves on to another activity. It is wonderful to see how proud and happy a two-year-old is when her chart is full. "I did it!" is a common cry for happy two-year-olds who feel they've done their share. An added bonus is her new, growing respect for your own work. A child who has her own responsibilities may more readily understand that you have to get chores done yourself.

THE TOY BOX
At Thirty-two Months

Glen has spent a long, fruitful morning playing with his blocks, train set, and a number of other toys. At eleven-thirty, he sits back on his heels, surveying his room. *Hungry!* he thinks. He doesn't know what time it is, but something tells him that the next event for the day is for him to sit at the kitchen table while Mom serves a peanut butter and jelly sandwich.

"Glen? Are you hungry?" Mom enters the room and stands beside him, looking at all he's done this morning. "Ready for a peanut butter sandwich?"

Glen's tummy rumbles in response, and he jumps up and tackles Mom in a bear hug. "Hungry!" he says.

"Okay," Mom says in a somewhat sterner voice. "But first we have to pick up some of these toys. What a mess it is in here!"

Glen steps back from his mom, confused. *But she said lunch!* he thinks. He sits down among his blocks. His hunger—combined with the discomfort caused by his mother's tone of voice—is about to overwhelm him, and he begins to cry. "Hungry!" he says.

"I know," his mom acknowledges, squatting down beside him. "It's lunchtime, and you want a sandwich. But you know that we have to clean up a little after playtime. Here, I'll help. I'll hold the block box, and you throw the blocks in."

At first, Glen refuses to cooperate. *Sandwich!* he reminds himself stubbornly, folding his arms and looking away. But Mom continues to hold the block box for him. "Where'd that helping boy go?" she says playfully, tossing in the first few blocks.

Glen likes the sound the blocks make. *My job!* he thinks. Quickly, he grabs some blocks and throws them in the box. With Mom's help, they're finished before he knows it.

"Good job, Glen," his mom says, picking him up. "We can put up the rest of the stuff later. Right now, let's go get you something to eat."

I did good, Glen tells himself with great satisfaction, giving his slightly neater room one last look over Mom's shoulder as she carries him out of the room. *Picked up blocks. Now I can eat!*

CHANGE CAN BE GOOD: MOVING
TOWARD NEW CHALLENGES

A year has passed, and Jane feels it has been an unusually trying but rewarding one. Owing to the fluke in her career trajectory that left her at home for the past twelve months, she has had the chance to spend a great deal more time with her daughter Annie than she'd ever expected. As week followed week, Jane began to get a sense of how important a predictable schedule and daily routines were to her daughter. Though she didn't want to go along with all of the routines that Annie's sitter had created, she and Annie have had a good time creating their own. Now Jane looks forward almost as much as Annie to rest time after lunch, when Jane reads her daughter several storybooks and Annie snuggles up against her mom. Annie loves "Freaky Friday," when she and her mom go off on a spontaneous adventure (a picnic in the park, a drive to the country), giving Annie a chance to be stimulated by new experiences and Jane a way to avoid cabin fever.

Now, as Annie looks forward to her third birthday, Jane considers the possibility of accepting a new job outside the home. She knows that taking the job would create yet another major change in Annie's life. But she believes that she knows better now how to prepare Annie for it—by talking about it frequently, demonstrating what will happen in concrete ways (such as showing Annie her new office and letting her draw pictures to decorate its walls), and understanding that even when Annie doesn't seem to be paying attention to what's happening she is really processing on some level what's going on. Fortunately, Annie's progress this year has somewhat reduced her need for everything to remain the same. She's even had a few new sitters since her first one left. Annie will start preschool this year, and her increasing interest in children her age will take some of the focus off Mom's activities. In fact, Jane looks forward to comparing notes with her daughter as they both venture out into a new group situation. If they can share their feelings about meeting new people, adjusting to new routines, and separating from one another, Jane hopes, they can both not only survive these major changes but actually thrive.

How the Need for Routine Evolves in the Third Year

24 MONTHS	Enjoys family routine
	Major changes (such as a new sibling or a move) may trigger regression
27 MONTHS	Need for order increases her attraction to routines
30 MONTHS	Likes accomplishing daily chores
	May show interest in using the potty
33 MONTHS	Grows more tolerant of minor disruptions in familiar routine
	Enjoys "discussing" plans for the day
36 MONTHS	Shows pride in her place as a full-fledged family member
	More willing to conform to family practices
	Shows increased interest in trying new things

FIRST-PERSON SINGULAR

In so many instances throughout this year and the next, conflicts between parent and child can be magnified or resolved with a simple change in routine. A stubborn refusal to lie still and go to sleep after the bedtime stories are finished, for example, may be remedied by playing a story on tape for your child to drift off to. As you work your way through this year, tinkering in one way or another with the routines that work best with your child, take notes on what works and what doesn't. Is your two-year-old the type who responds best to humor when she begins to feel overwhelmed, or does she need a hug and a quiet talk? Does she feel better when her routine is pretty much the same each day, or does she thrive on variety within a basic predictable framework? Does she experience "fads" during which she wants to do only one activity (play with clay) for days on end, and then switches allegiance abruptly to another activity (cutting with scissors) for the rest of the week?

Observing and taking notes on your child's attitudes toward routines can help you arrange her world so that she moves through it most effectively—the first step in teaching her to manage her environment more wisely by herself. A written record of what has worked and what hasn't in the past will save both of you time and effort in structuring her habits in the future.

READER'S NOTES

_____

_____

_____

_____

_____

_____

_____

_____

_____

_____

_____

_____

_____

_____

CHAPTER 8

"But I Want To!"— My Need for Limits

S tudies have shown that parents' consistency in limit-setting is much more important for toddlers than it is for infants.

It's seven in the evening when Mark hangs up the phone, and he hasn't even started dinner yet. He was late leaving work, got hung up at the child-care center when Lawrence, his two-year-old, insisted on showing him around the playhouse, and then had to stop by the grocery store. As soon as they got home, Mark dropped the groceries on the kitchen floor and collapsed on the living room sofa, while Lawrence wandered over to the television, switched it on, and sat down on the floor to watch.

Luckily, the television was tuned to the public station, because Mark was too exhausted to get up and change the channel. After an hour's rest, he managed to answer the phone when it rang. It was his wife, Mia, calling from her evening shift at the hospital. On opposite work schedules, she and Mark had hardly seen each other in three days, and it took them some time to catch up.

"Love you, too." Mark finally hangs up the phone and looks up with a dazed expression. *Wow. It's dark already,* he realizes. *Lawrence has been watching TV for . . .* he checks his watch . . . *one and a half hours!*

Guilt-stricken, Mark snaps off the television midprogram. "That's it, buddy," he says to his son. "Too much TV for one day. Come on. Dad needs help making supper."

"Whaaa . . . ?" Lawrence stares up at his father, stunned by his action. "I wanna watch TV!"

"That's enough TV!" Mark repeats. He hates it when Lawrence begs to watch television. It makes him feel like a bad parent. "Come on—I'll let you put the pasta in the water."

Mark strides off toward the kitchen, expecting Lawrence to follow him. Instead, the moment Mark's back is turned, Lawrence marches over to the television and turns it on. As the brightly colored figures reappear on the TV screen, Lawrence sits down on the floor again, very pleased with himself.

Mark hears the sound of the television and turns around. He can't believe Lawrence deliberately disobeyed him. His guilt increases as he marches back to turn the television off. *He's a complete addict!* he says to himself. "Young man, you will *not* turn the television on when I say the time is up," he snaps, grabbing Lawrence's arm and pulling him to his feet. "You come with me right now. We're cooking dinner, and you're helping." Mark starts back toward the kitchen, pulling Lawrence along with him.

Mark's insistence makes Lawrence all the more determined to have his way. "Let go!" he yells, and squirms out of his father's grasp. Before Mark can stop him, Lawrence races back to the television and turns it on, standing two inches in front of the screen exactly as his parents have always told him not to.

"That's it!" Mark's exhaustion rolls over him in a wave, and he feels himself lose control. He grabs Lawrence's hand and slaps it, hard. "*Bad* boy, Lawrence! Go to your room right now!"

Lawrence's eyes widen as he stares at his hand, then looks up at his dad. Mark has never hit him before, and Lawrence can hardly believe he did it now. Slowly, his expression changes from shock to fury. "Nyaaaa!" he yells, right in his father's face. Before Mark can react, Lawrence races away.

Mark starts to chase him, but then suddenly stops himself. *What am I doing?* he wonders, leaning against the wall. *Chasing a two-year-old around the house? Spanking him because I'm mad? I'm behaving worse than he is.*

Mark may deeply regret his actions toward his son, but at least he can remind himself that he's not alone in feeling pushed to the limit by such behavior. Few parenting challenges are more difficult than effectively managing the perfectly normal, healthy surges of defiance that all two-year-olds express on the road toward independence. It has often been said that age two offers a preview of what adolescence will be like. As you struggle with your child's bouts of rebellion, extreme emotion, and stubborn refusal to cooperate, you may agree. But as difficult as it is to believe for much of this year, your two-year-old's frequent misbehavior is a necessary step toward a valuable goal. Once he has tested the boundaries of his world—learned what the rules are, what will happen if he breaks them, and whether you will be there for him even when he's naughty—he can move beyond this chaotic phase toward greater self-confidence and self-discipline.

Your job, then, is to help your child come to respect these boundaries, reminding him what the limits are, teaching him to control his emotions, and explaining why certain behaviors are unacceptable. As your child moves through different phases of cognitive, verbal, and emotional development, this will not be an easy process. When rewarding his best efforts or responding to deliberate misbehavior, it's necessary to take into account his level of understanding, his particular temperament, his physical and emotional capacities, and your own emotional state at the moment. The parent of a two-year-old must understand that this is not the year to tell him to "clean up his room" (such a vague command only confuses and overwhelms him) or that his leaping about the kitchen is "driving you bananas" (he isn't ready to think about your feelings to that extent and will only puzzle over that interesting phrase), or to take him to the circus "because he's been good all month" (he can't remember details that far back or generalize in that way). On the other hand, his progress in cognitive development *will* increase his understanding that actions have consequences; his language skills will help him understand your explanations and express himself more often through words; and his longer memory will help him remember what's off limits and what's okay. As the year progresses, his ability to control his emotions will improve, and new feelings of empathy will begin to curb some of his more aggressive behavior. The key to maneuvering through this difficult period lies in keeping your rules or commands simple and specific, noting which responses work best during each particular phase, changing your methods to suit new situations, and keeping in mind your long-term goal—a confident, aware, *self*-disciplined child.

A PARENT'S STORY
"No, Timmy! Hot!"

"My daughter, Zoe, is a real handful," a colleague told me at a conference recently. "She's constantly getting into one fix or another, and when she was two, she was so physically active that I was never sure she even heard me when I tried to explain how she should behave. She'd grab another kid's toy and run off with it before I could deal with the situation. I remember how upset I used to get, thinking that she was going to grow up to become a selfish brat and everyone was going to blame me.

"Then, about the time she turned three, there was this total change in her behavior. She started getting interested in how other kids acted, and she loved to tell them when they were doing something wrong. I still remember how happy she sounded saying, 'No, no, Timmy, hot!' whenever the little neighbor boy came within a foot of our stove. She loved to tell her best friend, Sheila, that sharing made everybody feel better, and she got to be a real stickler for whose turn it was when I played board games with her. Of course, we made a lot of jokes about what a dictator she was turning out to be (and we did have to teach her to tone down the bossiness a bit), but it was great to know she'd been *listening* to me all those years—or at least that she'd learned something from hanging out with other kids. Once I saw that she recognized bad behavior, I was able to talk with her more about her own manners. She got a lot better about following the rules over the next couple of years. I guess I just had to wait for her physical energy to slow down some and for her listening ability to improve.

"Two is a hard year because other people's kids always seem to 'get' the idea of following rules before yours does, and then you feel like a failure as a parent. But all you really need to do, I think, is stay consistent and keep the faith. It's hard to believe it, but two doesn't last forever."

"THAT'S THE RULE": SETTING CLEAR LIMITS TO LIVE BY

As you race from one discipline crisis ("Ray, give Sarah back her doll!") to another ("Ray, no jumping on the bed!"), you can be forgiven for believing that your two-year-old invented the concept of testing limits this year, but the fact is that he has been experimenting with his behavior and your responses to it practically from birth. Back then, as you cuddled him when he smiled and looked unhappy when he yelled, your infant came to understand which behavior created the best results. As the year progressed and you rewarded his positive social interactions, good eating habits, and more adaptable sleep patterns, he continued to learn what the limits were in each of these areas and molded his behavior to meet them to some degree. Only when he had learned to crawl and then to walk, however, did the two of you begin to encounter classic limit-setting situations. As your one-year-old began to interact with a wider range of objects and people, you responded more often with, "Don't touch that," "Good boy," and, "Say thank you." Your words and actions intrigued him, stimulating his developing interest in the ways your attitudes differed from his. He became fascinated by your concept of limits and began to experiment with ways of figuring out where they were exactly and whether you responded in the same way every time to these experiments.

Now, in his third year, your child's cognitive, physical, and emotional development have come together to enable him to concentrate more on the issue of limits. This can be extremely trying, of course, but it also presents a wonderful opportunity to *teach* him more about his world. By accepting your two-year-old's many behavioral blunders as necessary steps in acquiring a new skill—rather than as attempts to embarrass you in public or drive you out of your mind—you can take advantage of this window of opportunity. Look back on how you might have felt the first time you ate at a traditional Japanese restaurant—did you know to take your shoes off, to sit on the floor, and use chopsticks? Did you apply the right sauces to the right foods? Your two-year-old must learn to cope with an equally bewildering array of rules, expectations, and unspoken conventions. He needs your help.

The keys to success in this teaching activity are to *keep it simple* and *be consistent.* Just as you had to start with the basics when entering the Japanese restaurant ("Where do I put my shoes?"), your child needs to start with the simplest rules before he can expand his thinking to more general concepts. By speaking in simple, concrete ways that your two-year-old can understand, you make it possible for him to succeed at obeying and create a positive cycle in which he *wants* to follow the rules to win your approval.

Increasingly, part of making rules comprehensible will include explaining *why* they should be followed (always at a level he can understand). Your child's experiments with the concept of cause and effect have already taught him that his actions have consequences, and he will remain fascinated by this fact throughout this year. You can use his interest to help him focus on proper behavior by linking action and consequence as closely as possible. It's good to tell your young two-year-old, "Don't take Harold's toy," rather than, "Be nice to Harold"—but as he moves through the year it becomes even more effective to say, "Look, you took Harold's toy, and now he's crying. Give him back the toy so he'll feel better. Here's another toy for you." Your child may not want to cooperate with your instructions—he may not even appear to understand

To best capture your two-year-old's attention, try to set brief, consistent limits—ideally made face to face.

them at first—but with repetition he will gradually begin to comprehend the reasons behind your behavioral rules. Of course, some restrictions—particularly those involving your child's safety—are too important to wait for your child to achieve a thorough understanding of them. Fortunately, your child is old enough to accept the fact that he can't run into the street or wander off at the shopping mall because "that's the rule." Gradually, you will be able to shorten your more common demands to code phrases. Simply saying, "Parking lot," as you get out of your car at the mall will remind your child to hold your hand as you walk across the lot, refrain from running, and look both ways before crossing the street.

Maintaining a close link between actions and their consequences is important in responding to your child's behavior as well. His cognitive skills and memory are not sufficiently developed for him to think about and analyze his past actions very well. To create a mental link between his behavior and its results, then, it's important to respond immediately and clearly. When your child takes a playmate's toy, explain *at that moment* that he should give it back (and why), rather than waiting until after the play date is over. As MRI studies have shown, your words routinely create new neuronal connections in your child, and strengthen old ones. In other words, they literally shape his brain.

When responding to misbehavior, try to keep your response factual and instructive, rather than emotional and judgmental. Though it's true that your negative response is always a good motivator for your child to change his immediate behavior (particularly as he approaches age three and grows more interested in pleasing you), shouting at him or calling him a "bad boy" will only distract him from the lesson you really want him to learn (not to take toys from other children). Instead, add a brief, matter-of-fact, "I don't like it when you take other children's toys away." (Make sure, however, that you just as readily say, "I like it when you share.") It also helps to look at the situation from your child's point of view. After all, taking away a playmate's toy means that he has the toy—a very powerful motivator for a two-year-old. To start to override this, point out to him that "See, you got the toy for a second, but then Mommy took it away. Grabbing toys from people is not the way to keep a toy. Next time, ask for the toy, and if he gives it to you, you can play with it."

"LISTEN TO ME!": ADJUSTING YOUR STYLE TO SUIT YOUR CHILD

As with every other aspect of parenting a young child, your knowledge of your two-year-old's unique temperament is one of your best tools in setting effective limits. A very active child may not hear you if you ask him to "stop it" and may need a touch on the arm or direct eye contact before he can pay attention. A sensitive child may crumble when you express your disapproval and respond to your instruction only when it's couched in the most positive language. A child who cries easily will need a moment to master his emotions before he can focus on what you are trying to say. A child who is shy or easily embarrassed may need privacy when you talk to him.

Even a child's "family temperament" has an effect on which techniques work best for him. A child whose family interacts in more dramatic, extraverted ways would probably expect, or at least be less fazed by, a more emotional response to his misbehavior. A child with highly verbal parents may respond better to logical explanation and negotiation and resist the statement, "That's the rule." For these reasons, it's best to listen to the general advice of child-care experts and other experienced parents, and then tailor that advice to your child's specific needs and circumstances, and your own.

Once you have decided which kinds of responses work best for your child at this particular point in his development, keep your responses as consistent as possible. As difficult as it is sometimes to refuse your child a snack at bedtime when he didn't eat much supper, and awkward as it can be to enforce a rule in the middle of a birthday party or other public event, consistency is the key to developing good habits and (eventually) reducing the number of conflicts you and your child experience. Keep in mind that on an unconscious level your child is monitoring the number of times his behavior (crying for candy) leads to a desirable response (getting the candy) and how many times it leads to an undesirable one (refusal to give in and provide a treat). Just as your frequent smiles encouraged his happy expressions as an infant, your *consistent* responses now will mold his actions in the future. Though there is always room for the occasional exception (he can have candy before lunch this time), in general each time you say, "Okay, just this once," you set him back a bit in his progress toward desirable behavior.

Studies have shown that parents' consistency in limit-setting is much more important for toddlers than it is for infants. Just as important as one parent's consistency is the level of consistency between both parents' approaches. Parents should agree this year not to undermine each other's rules and parenting style. Two-year-olds easily pick up on the differences between their parents' approaches to discipline and are able to use these disagreements to get around restrictions. We have all seen older children who have developed this skill to a fine art.

Of course, it's easy for parents to acknowledge that they need to decide on a single parenting style, but much harder to go along with a partner's methods when one passionately disagrees. Our parenting philosophies usually depend a great deal on how we were raised ourselves—whether we're inspired by those memories or are reacting against them. Our intense recollections of how we felt when certain methods were used ("When Mom sent me to my room, I thought she didn't love me") make it especially difficult to discuss these matters objectively. As you try to work out with your partner a "game plan" for limit-setting, keep in mind that your child will be capable of accommodating differences in your attitudes to some degree. (Experiencing moderately different styles that aren't in direct opposition can even be a good experience.) It is more damaging when one parent contradicts, sabotages, or ridicules the other parent's techniques in front of the child. Keep your emotions out of the discussion as much as you possibly can, and don't debate parental techniques in front of your child. When designing a parental strategy on which you can both agree, start with your general philosophies and work toward specific strategies. Try to reach a compromise on the important issues *before* you begin to enforce them frequently. Avoid getting hung up on each other's inflammatory buzzwords ("You're too permissive," "You're too strict"), and focus on identifying which approaches actually work best with your child at this point in his development. The sooner you find a way to settle such disagreements the better, since the same disputes are likely to come up again and again throughout your life with your child.

As your child approaches his third birthday and socializes more frequently with other children, he'll begin to realize that rules vary widely from family to family. Comparing and judging these different approaches to discipline is a favorite activity for some children—and a sign that he's accepting your own rules as part of "how his family is." The clearer and more consistent you can be about your rules, and the more consistently you can enforce them, the firmer your child's footing will be as he tries out his learned behavior in the larger world.

When Parents Disagree

"I wish Scott and I had compared parenting philosophies before we got engaged," a friend once said to me. "If I knew then what kinds of fights we would have about how to raise the kids, and how hard it would be on our children, I don't think I would have married him." Certainly, few issues run so deep, and linger as long, as fundamental disagreements over how to raise a child. Still, even if you and your partner find yourselves on opposite ends of the parenting spectrum, there are ways to make it easier to design a viable strategy.

First, it is important to back away from the kinds of global statements that do little more than set you up in opposition to one another. Claiming that you believe in "setting a child free to be creative" will only alienate a parent who believes in "obedience and proper behavior." Instead, look for some small areas in which it's possible to compromise, even if the large issues remain unresolved. Agree to let your child choose her first chores, for instance, and agree to make sure she does them. Discuss specific situations until you've agreed exactly how to address them ("When Ralph wants ice cream and he hasn't eaten all his dinner, we'll insist that he take one more bite and finish his milk before he can have dessert"). Talk about ways in which each of your deepest parenting convictions can be carried out in real, day-to-day life ("I don't believe in spanking. If you feel the urge to spank Ralph, give him a time-out and let me take over"). Decide what to do when a new issue comes up and only one of you is present ("Handle it within our general guidelines, and we'll discuss it alone as soon as I get home"). Most important, use your home life as a miniature lab experiment: Observe your child's response to a particular parenting technique, review the response with your partner, and use your new knowledge to help design more techniques that will work best with your particular child.

With frequent reminders to one another that you share a common goal (a well-brought-up child) and that your love for him is what motivates you both, you are likely to get better at such compromises over time. If your conversations fail to improve the situation over the course of the year, however—or if you and your partner just can't seem to discuss the matter—this is a time to think seriously about obtaining outside guidance, whether it's a parents' support group, a professionally run workshop, or family counseling. Discipline issues will continue to arise throughout your parenting careers. Your child will benefit greatly from your determined efforts to settle on a game plan early in his life.

"I TAKE TURNS LIKE BEN!": THE POWER OF IMITATION

Fortunately, your child's very strong urge to imitate is even more powerful when it comes to family members than it is with other children. Given a choice between imitating your behavior and a neighbor child's, your child will (eventually) settle on yours. Setting a good example for your child becomes one of the most effective means of shaping his behavior and enforcing limits.

Sometime around your child's second birthday, he probably became much more interested in observing other children and began to enjoy imitating their behavior. At first, this imitation was practically his only way of interacting with others—he signaled his interest in another child by mimicking whatever action or noise that child happened to make. Soon he began to imitate other children's more general behavior as well, both in their presence and later, when he was on his own. Often this was a good thing—many two-year-olds have learned to hold a crayon correctly, count to ten, and even use the toilet simply by imitating the children in their lives. Sometimes, of course, the results were not so good—as when your child began hitting other children after playing with a child who hit.

If your two-year-old has learned to hit by watching the child next door, you can show him how to settle differences in more positive ways, and then consistently demonstrate your methods through your own behavior. Studies have shown that setting a good example themselves is one of the most effective ways in which parents socialize a young child. Though it's only human to notice most often your child's negative imitations, work at noting and praising his positive imitations, too.

During this third year, your child will begin to respond to many other influences in his world. It's extremely important to take into account the examples offered by television, movies, and other adults. Rather than ignoring these influences, or trying to shield him from them completely (an impossible task), use them as opportunities to discuss in simple terms your reasons for requiring that he behave differently. Certainly, as he nears his third birthday, your child is old enough to understand that you don't approve of punching people like the cartoon characters on TV because "it isn't good to hurt people." Keep in mind that young children really don't understand the difference between fake and real violence. As you watch a program with him, comment on the behavior you see ("Oh-oh, that's going to get him into trouble"). Narrate what you would do if you were in the same situation ("Wow, that guy needs a time-out"). By hearing you observe and comment on different modes of behavior, he will gradually learn to judge the behavior he witnesses instead of blindly imitating it—a valuable skill to acquire for later life.

THE TOY BOX
At Thirty-six Months

Grace's twin cousins, four-year-old Will and Ryan, have come for a visit, and Grace is proudly showing them the objects in her toy basket in the family room. Will and Ryan are very active boys, and Grace increasingly finds herself pushed to the side as they pull out and toss away toy cars, rag dolls, dress-up clothes, and several varieties of blocks. "Look, a train!" Ryan says, spotting the box of train tracks and cars wedged behind the basket. He pulls it out, opens the box, and starts setting up the equipment. Meanwhile, Will has found a soft ball and begins bouncing it against the piano.

"No, no, Will," Grace says to her cousin. "No throwing!" Will continues to throw the ball. "It's fun," he tells Grace. "Here, you try it."

Will hands the ball to Grace. She's tempted to throw it at the piano. It makes a nice, solid *thud* when it hits the wood. Besides, she's thrilled that Will, a big kid, has offered to play with her. But Grace can't shake a vague idea of what her mother might do if she sees what they're doing. In the end, Grace wanders away from Will, still holding the ball and still shaking her head no. "My turn," she says to Ryan, squatting down to play with the train set. She smiles to herself. Mom, watching from the doorway, is pleasantly surprised. Grace didn't like Will's behavior, and so she broke the cycle of imitation in the only way she knew how—by leaving the scene.

"GOOD FOR YOU!": REWARDING GOOD BEHAVIOR

If you have ever worked for a boss who criticized your performance constantly without showing you how you *should* do your job, you may understand the frustration a two-year-old feels practically every day. Confused about proper behavior, often too overwhelmed emotionally to behave in positive ways, told to "stop that" several times a day or even several times an hour, it's little wonder that children this age are known for their tantrums, defiance, and other forms of emotional meltdown. You can improve your child's morale—thus making him *want* to behave well—by praising his efforts in ways he can understand. Again, the best kinds of responses to good behavior are simple and immediate. A simple "Good job," when your child completes a chore may work better than a longer analysis ("I'm so proud of you for picking up your blocks. You clean up your room better than anyone I know. I bet you'll be a very neat person when you grow up") because it doesn't distract him with tangential thoughts or emotions. Two is a good age to begin awarding stickers on a chart listing four or more positive behaviors you expect. By putting a gold star next to the heading "Clean up Room," you teach your child to take pride in his accomplishments and inspire him to continue behaving well. Promising a treat or activity in exchange for good behavior really isn't a bribe, no matter what your friends say. It's an acceptable form of conditioning that will help your child figure out how to accomplish good behavior, and it won't "spoil" your child as long as you don't promise a treat for *every* act of compliance every time. In general, rewards do not have to be as consistent as other responses to behavior—your child doesn't have to get a gold star every time he cleans his room for gold stars to be effective. (In fact, research has shown that sporadic reinforcement is the most effective method.) But they should occur frequently enough for your child to understand that you are focusing on his behavior and that you appreciate his compliance.

Stickers and treats make for wonderful rewards at this age, because they are concrete objects that your child can look at or hold in his hand. Still, the most powerful reward he can receive at any age is your attention and approval. As you keep your focus on your child's positive behavior and ignore some of his less acceptable actions, you may well see those negative behaviors diminishing steadily as the year goes by. Children—even two-year-olds—want more than anything for their parents to approve of them. Of course, there will be times when simple positive reinforcement isn't enough to ensure that your child behaves safely and responsibly. As pointed out earlier in this chapter, firmness and consistency have their place, and there are even times when "because that's the rule" is the best way to guarantee good behavior. In the long run, however, your goal for your child should center on teaching him to control his own behavior, rather than following someone else's arbitrary rules. To this end, showing your child that you like what he's doing—and helping him understand what's in it for him—is one of the best ways to encourage him to set limits for himself.

Q & A
Naughty, Naughty

Q: Since before I ever even had any children, I've believed in the idea of positive discipline. I always thought that if I were firm and set a good example for my kid, he would learn to behave like I did. But my two-and-a-half-year-old daughter, Eileen, is such a pill nearly all the time. If I put her in her car seat, she tries to unbuckle it. If I take her to a movie, she makes so much noise that we have to leave. If I take her to the playground, she hits another kid with a sand toy. I know she's two and it's expected that she'll misbehave sometimes. But I end up practically in tears by the end of every day. Am I going to have to start spanking her?

A: You're right when you acknowledge that all two-year-olds misbehave, but you're wrong if you think spanking is the magic answer. Misbehaving is part of the process of learning limits and growing up. If your daughter's behavior is starting to overwhelm you, there are some steps you can take to improve the situation this year. First, try to make it as easy as possible for her to behave *well*. Part of this process involves praising her when she does meet your expectations, but it also includes very simple practical considerations, such as providing her with a toy to play with while she's in her car seat, or removing the knife from her setting at a restaurant before she smashes it against her plate. Avoid situations that are beyond her ability to cope with now, such as movies, large crowds, or long separations from you. Consider her physical and emotional state as you plan her day. If she didn't get enough sleep

Stickers or a similar reward system are valuable positive reinforcements as you "catch your child being good."

last night, skip the trip to the playground—she won't have the emotional control to deal with other children. If she's hungry, cut the visit to your mother's short and go home for lunch, where you know you'll have fewer eating problems.

Sometimes when our two-year-olds' misbehavior has us down, we wonder whether all of our parenting strategies are completely misguided. Often, however, it turns out that our mistakes are in the details. And we may find ourselves, despite our best efforts, attending only to the negative behaviors we want to correct. Acknowledging your child's progress, keeping an eye on her shifting capabilities and preparing for her needs will help you smooth the journey toward age three.

"TIME OUT!": CREATING EFFECTIVE CONSEQUENCES FOR BAD BEHAVIOR

However much you encourage good behavior in your child, there will be plenty of instances—probably several each day—when he violates the rules of conduct you've created for him. At these times, try to keep in mind that testing your limits truly is one of his most important activities this year—part of his struggle to be more independent. Much as he seems to rebel against your rules, however, it is vital for you to show him that you expect him to comply with them. Only in this way can his world begin to take shape, with parameters for behavior on which he can rely.

As in all aspects of setting limits, the best approach is a matter-of-fact focus on cause and effect rather than a global condemnation ("Bad boy!") or an emotional response ("How could you do such a thing?!"). Keep your responses to misbehavior simple and specific, and make sure the consequences occur immediately after the action. Negative consequences will be even more effective if they proceed naturally from your child's actions. If he throws his food on the floor in a fit of rage during dinner, for example, you might respond by calmly cleaning up the mess and then refusing to give him a treat. (As he approaches age three, it even makes sense to have him help with the cleaning.) By refusing to share his anger and making the consequences both consistent and just, you will eventually convince your child that there's little satisfaction in misbehaving.

A common mistake I see parents of two-year-olds making is expecting their child to have a greater ability to self-regulate than he's capable of at his stage of development. Though it's true that your child can understand the words "stop that" when he's breaking every crayon he has in half, he isn't necessarily able to come up with a way to stop his activity once he's started it. He may not even understand the problem—maybe he thinks that he's providing himself with twice as many crayons! By substituting an alternative activity (getting out the felt-tipped markers and suggesting he draw a picture of his cat), you can help him escape a bad situation while teaching him positive ways to change his behavior.

It's also important to limit your "No's" so that your child doesn't feel overwhelmed by the sheer number of rules he has to follow. Start with the most important issues involving safety and the protection of important property, and work your way gradually down your list toward the details of good manners and social behavior. Working on only a few issues at a time helps your child feel that good behavior is possible. By arranging his environment so that he has fewer opportunities to misbehave (limiting his choice of activities, diverting him while you dress him or brush his teeth, keeping dangerous objects out of reach), you limit his "failures" to a manageable number and help him believe that he is a "good boy" overall.

When your child does misbehave, consider his developmental level as you respond. A two-year-old's sense of time is quite different from an adult's. A two-minute time-out will feel like two hours to him. Use a timer that beeps at the end to let him know when his time out is over. After the time-out, be sure you explain—clearly, simply, and without undue emotion—why he had to be alone for a while. Point out that it's his behavior you disapproved of, not him. Tell him you're sure he'll do better next time—that everyone makes mistakes and the important thing is that we learn from them. Then give him a quick hug to let him know that you love him no matter how he behaves. If your child responds with anger or defiance, don't be too concerned. Committing a "crime" and being punished is a disorienting experience for a two-year-old. In trying to reestablish his sense of self-control, he may feel the need to tell the world, "This is how I am—like it or not!" If you've ever resisted a hug from your partner after an argument, you may understand how he feels.

A CHILD'S-EYE VIEW
The Other Side of the Door

Eva, who's nearly three, is bored. Her mom's on the phone, and her six-year-old brother, Nicholas, is in his room with a friend. Eva wanders over to her brother's room and stands in the doorway, watching the boys arm up with water pistols for an outdoor game. "I want one," she says, walking over to grab a water gun.

"No way!" Nicholas shouts, grabbing the toy and holding it out of her reach. "You can't play with us, Eva. Go away!"

Meanie, Eva thinks. *I want to play, too.* "Gimme that!" she yells, reaching for the water gun. When Nicholas refuses, she starts to scream.

"Eva, you stop that noise this instant!" Mommy is standing in the doorway, looking very mad. "Come on out of Nicholas's room. He wants to play with his friend right now."

Eva is unhappy that Mommy's not agreeing with her. She remembers how boring it is outside this room, wandering around the house by herself. *Don't want to go,* she decides. Unable to keep her impulses in check, she has to move. "My turn!" she yells at her mother, and grabs the gun from her brother.

"All right, young lady. That's it. You're having a time-out!" Eva's mother marches her to her own room. "Stay here for two minutes," she says. "I said no. There's no screaming in this house. I want you to think about how much your screaming hurts people's ears."

The door slams, and Eva finds herself alone in her room. This is even worse than before! She smashes the door with her fist, but there's no response. She starts to cry and sits on the floor. *Hate being alone!* she thinks as tears run down her face. *Bad Mommy! Bad Nicholas!* The sounds of the boys running outside to play only make her cry louder.

When Mom opens the door, Eva's still out of sorts. She doesn't want to listen to Mom tell her about her bad behavior. She sniffs, wipes her nose on her sleeve, and stalks into the playroom. The plastic knight's helmet, sword, and shield her daddy gave her rest invitingly against the wall. Eva picks up the sword and waves it around with great satisfaction. *My sword!* She whacks a nearby sofa a few times with the sword, enjoying a new sense of power. "Give me that gun!" she demands, and whacks the bed again.

"DON'T HIT ME!": AVOIDING THE TRAPS OF PHYSICAL PUNISHMENT

"How many times have I *told* you not to hit other kids?!" *Whack.* What parent hasn't felt the temptation to respond this way when their child strikes out physically for the umpteenth time? Perhaps you've thought, if only fleetingly, "If a *grown-up* talked to me like my child just did, I'd want to punch him in the mouth!" The fact is, however, that two-year-olds are not at all like grown-ups. Not only do they have very little concept of the effects of their actions and words, but physical punishment such as a slap or spanking violates their still extremely fragile sense of self, smashing apart their sense of how the world works in ways that no adult can completely understand. Clearly, such an experience eclipses any behavioral lesson the punishment was meant to give. What it does teach children is that aggression is an acceptable way to control others—in other words, as countless studies have shown in recent decades, it teaches children to hit back. In fact, I've never met a parent who felt good about having spanked a child—justified, yes, but not good.

As difficult as it is to control our own behavior when a two-year-old lashes out for what seems to be no reason or misbehaves in the same way for the two-hundredth time, refraining from physical punishment is one of the most important goals this year. Keep in mind that your two-year-old is *testing* your responses, and do your best to pass that test. Think in advance about the positive ways you'd like to see your child respond when he is frustrated or angry, and set a good example by responding in those ways yourself. Be aware of the times when you or your child are feeling stressed or otherwise vulnerable, and try to avoid confrontations or challenges at those times. Plan your environment in ways that discourage physical aggression—maintaining clear, nonphysical consequences for misbehavior, taking time away from your child when you're beginning to feel burned out, and sharing your frustration with other adults rather than taking it out on your child.

Ironically, one of the reasons parents today may feel pushed to react *physically* to a child's behavior is the popular belief that setting strict *verbal* limits stifles young children's self-expression and leads to lowered self-esteem. It is easy to worry that saying no too often will prevent our children from learning to negotiate and from feeling free to share their feelings with us. As a result, we may grit our teeth and put up with a great deal more whining, arguing, or defiance than we would like to— until the moment when we are pushed past our tolerance level and simply blow up. If you find this to be the case, consider how much better it would be to decide ahead of time how much negative behavior you can tolerate, firmly tell your child no well before you reach the point of no return, and put up with his inevitable angry response while you are still able to control your temper.

As important as it is to encourage children to express themselves fully, setting clear and even strict limits is not a bad thing. Limits help your child build internal controls that will fortify him throughout life. Point out to him that grown-ups have to follow rules, too. Give him examples ("Mom was mad, but she didn't yell"). By demonstrating your own conscious, thoughtful ways of preventing and controlling your own outbursts of anger, you will show him that physical aggression is not the answer. By keeping limits in your lives together, you will not only enjoy a more tolerable day-to-day life with your two-year-old but teach him the value and methods of *self*-discipline—which, of course, is every parent's ultimate goal.

IF YOU'RE CONCERNED
Controlling Your Own Anger

When your child loses control of herself and refuses to listen to reason, the urge to strike out physically can be overwhelming. What begins as a firm hand on her shoulder ends with a sharp twist or an angry shake; what starts out as a lesson in logical consequences ("This is what hitting feels like! Do you like that?") ends with shock and tears on your child's part and horrible feelings of guilt and regret for you. Ironically, the best way to avoid losing control of yourself with your child is the same way you help her control her own behavior—by heading off difficult situations whenever possible and by monitoring your emotional state and implementing simple, concrete solutions for the times when you're past your tolerance level. A great deal of conflict occurs, for example, when parents try to cram more activities into the day than their young children can keep up with. By *underestimating* how much you can get done and leaving more than enough preparation time, you can avoid those moments of desperation when you realize you're late to an appointment and your child insists on playing with her tea set instead of putting on her shoes. Other problems occur when we expect too much from a child at a certain point in her development—proper behavior from a curious toddler at a relative's house, for example, or adult-type patience while shopping, eating in a restaurant, or waiting in line. Relaxing your expectations and remembering that your child has not had even three full years to learn all the rules may help you maintain equilibrium as your child stomps on Grandma's foot, spreads her toys all over the living room, or punches the ATM buttons *again* when you just told her not to. It is also important to remember that you, your partner, and the rest of the family need scheduled time away from your child. A life dedicated wholly to satisfying a two-year-old's demands would send nearly any parent over the brink.

No matter how careful you are to build relaxation into your lifestyle, however, your child is bound to inspire your anger now and then. Your goal at these times is to know when you've passed your own tolerance level and to choose from one of several ways to back off. A client of mine once told me she makes a point of not touching her child at all when she's angry. "I read once that a good way to discipline a child is to take them by the arm and lead them physically through what you want them to do, since it's easier for them to learn by doing stuff than by hearing about it," she said. "But I noticed that when I did that—marching Carol into the bathroom and actually guiding her hand to brush her teeth—it was really easy for me to lose control of my anger and *jerk* her really meanly through the process instead. She would say, "Mom, you're hurting me." I just couldn't trust myself to be gentle when I was mad at her, so instead I learned to put my hands behind my back or in my pockets, breathe deeply, and talk her through it instead."

In general, it's a good idea to avoid trying to discipline your child when you yourself feel out of control. At these times, you're not likely to discipline well or wisely, and you may well find yourself unable to avoid physical action. Instead, give yourself a time-out. If necessary, avoid touching your child, as my client did. Shut yourself up in the bathroom for a minute if you have to. Call a sympathetic friend to substitute for you, and go for a short drive. You'll find that your sense of reason returns very quickly given the chance—and you will have avoided actions that you would later regret.

"LET'S START OVER":
MOVING BEYOND DISCIPLINE

Is family life always going to be this exhausting? Mark arrives home with Lawrence, now nearly three, so tired he can barely fit his key into the lock of the front door. Once inside, he drops onto the living room sofa while Lawrence putters around the room as usual. "So—how was your day?" he asks his son, putting his feet up on the coffee table. "Did you play with the big boys today?"

"Uh . . . no," Lawrence says distractedly. "Daddy, can I watch TV?"

Mark appreciates the fact that Lawrence at least stuck to their agreement that he would ask to watch television instead of just switching the TV on. They've talked a lot about this issue over the past year, and Lawrence seems to understand now that he needs permission to watch a show or two a day. For a while near the beginning of the year, Mark tried to cut out television altogether, but he had to accept the fact that he is just too tired at the end of the workday to start interacting directly with a young child right away. A half-hour show gives him the time he needs to unwind and lets Lawrence feel that he has some say in what he does at home. Lately, Mark has noticed that watching the show with Lawrence, and talking with him about the characters and what they're doing, is a good way to phase into the evening's activities. As Lawrence has gotten better at expressing himself through language, their conversations have become more interesting. Mark actually feels closer to his son as they talk about the issues raised on the show.

"Okay, pal, that's it," Mark says 30 minutes later as the show's credits roll. He gets up quickly and turns off the television—having learned not to let Lawrence focus on the ad for the next show. "I brought some paper clips home from the office," he says. "Do you know how to make a paper-clip chain? Come on, I'll show you how." Mark knows now that distracting Lawrence helps him make the transition from TV to another activity. Stringing paper clips will keep him busy at the kitchen table while Mark makes dinner.

"But, Daddy . . . ," Lawrence says, reaching longingly for the TV.

"Look, here are the paper clips," Mark repeats, pulling them out of his pocket. "Come on. I'll race you to the table!"

To his surprise, Lawrence takes him up on his challenge. All in all, he has to admit that parenting Lawrence has gotten easier over the past few months. Lawrence seems less rebellious and more committed to trying to please his dad. He's learned some basic behavior that takes the pressure off their relationship. Best of all, he's accepting some of the house rules that Mark feels are most important. A couple of times, Mark has even watched Lawrence stop himself from misbehaving instead of waiting for his dad to distract him, correct him, or otherwise help him change direction. Of course, not every day is as easy as this one when they get home, but the easier days seem to happen more and more often.

ADVANCES
Moving Toward Self-discipline in the Third Year

24 MONTHS	Begins to understand simple time-related concepts ("soon," "after breakfast," etc.)
	Learns a great deal of behavior through imitation
27 MONTHS	Starts to rely more on words to communicate feelings
	More attentive to parents' commands
30 MONTHS	Behavior becomes more logical, less randomly defiant
	Remembers behavioral rules more easily
33 MONTHS	Increasingly eager to please parents and be a "good boy"
	Somewhat better able to wait for what he wants
36 MONTHS	Observes others' behavior and compares it to his own

Can follow a two- or three-part command

Starts to experiment with negotiation

FIRST-PERSON SINGULAR

Every child responds to various limit-setting techniques in his own unique way. By observing your child's responses and trying to understand the feelings that inspire them, you can better tailor your discipline techniques to suit him. Write down which techniques you have tried and what the results were. At what times of day, or on what days of the week, is it most difficult for your child to behave well? Which of his behaviors threaten to send you over the edge, and what have you done to remedy this situation? When your child reveals in his own words how he feels when you respond to his behavior, record his words here. He will be interested to know what went through his mind as a two-year-old, and you'll be able to refer to his refreshingly honest comments in the years to come.

READER'S NOTES

_____

_____

_____

_____

_____

_____

_____

_____

_____

_____

_____

_____

_____

_____

_____

_____

_____

_____

_____

_____

CHAPTER 9

Looking Ahead—I'm Three

O ne of the greatest leaps your child will take next year will be in the realm of her imagination.

What an eventful year this has been for the children we've observed in these chapters and for you and your family. Over the past twelve months, Amy and Kaisha, Dylan and Jeff—and your two-year-old as well—have learned to skip, turn a somersault, and hold a pencil; to enjoy an interesting conversation; to share (sometimes) with friends; and to use predictable daily routines as a base for further exploration. We have watched their unique personalities assert themselves as they learned to express their feelings more clearly, use imaginary play to work out conflicts, and creatively resist the rules and restrictions they did not like. Your own development as a parent has been no less impressive as your time spent playing with your child and observing her actions showed you new ways to shape and encourage her growth. This expanded knowledge will support you through the next year as you witness the continued blossoming of your three-year-old's fascinating personality. Next year an array of skills she has worked so hard to develop will come together at last, creating a whole that is truly far greater than the sum of its parts. The more you understand your two-year-old today, the more you will be able to enhance and enjoy this next step in her growth.

"WHO ARE YOU? WHO AM I?": WHAT YOUR CHILD HAS LEARNED

Verbal and emotional growth dominated your child's development this year, though giant steps were certainly also taken in other areas. This has been the year when your child really began to talk to you—picking up new phrases, words, and inflections at a breathtaking rate and gradually substituting language for tears and physical expression. As the months passed, she grew more confident that, with language, she could control at least a limited part of her world (negotiating for a later bathtime, explaining why your actions made her sad). Her moments of defiance probably decreased over the course of this year, and she began to interact in more reasonable ways. By her third birthday, the two of you have probably worked out a number of verbal formulas—a special rhyme while brushing her teeth, an exchange of thoughts at bedtime—to get her through her daily routines and inevitable emotional roadblocks. In the future, as your voice takes its place in her own inner dialogue, she will learn to use similar techniques to encourage herself and manage her emotional ups and downs.

Your two-year-old's emotional dramas were strongly linked this year to her need to establish herself as a presence in her world. As her language skills enabled her to express newly hatched opinions and desires, she experienced a strong urge to see that her opinions were recognized and her desires realized. No doubt her insistence on "doing it herself" or having her own way sometimes had you tearing out your hair in frustration. But such interactions ideally also sparked new, creative methods for the two of you to compromise and get along. Now, as the year ends, your child has a clearer idea of where you stand on behavioral issues, what her limits are, and how she can please you while still, whenever possible, achieving her goals. She has found ways to establish her presence beyond simply stomping her foot and shouting, "No!" She has learned that sharing, taking turns, listening to others, and other prosocial behaviors win her the attention she craves. Gradually, over the year to come, she will experiment with these new ideas to carve out a place for herself in the wider world of social interaction.

Of course, none of this verbal, emotional, and social growth would have been possible without a great deal of cognitive development over the past year. By piecing together bits of knowledge gained from careful observation, your two-year-old began working to create a coherent understanding of how her world works and the meaning behind certain events. Her theories often led to amusing misconceptions (candles at dinner don't necessarily mean it's your birthday), but day by day her accuracy improved. As she became more aware of the currents of emotion, adult conversations, and other fluctuating elements surrounding her, she experienced new fears and anxieties. Fortunately, an expanding imaginative ability allowed her to begin working her fears out through her play. Now, on the brink of turning three, your child is much more familiar with the world of ideas. She is able to remember and think about events that occurred quite a long time ago. She can use logic to some extent to negotiate for what she wants. She can puzzle over problems and come up with solutions, all in her mind. In the next year, this ability to "hold her world in her head" will come to fruition. She will be able to recognize symbols, such as numbers and letters, written with a crayon. She will draw an actual shape or a face instead of simply scribbling with a crayon. Her "magical thinking" will increase dramatically, and she will come up with fascinating answers to such questions as, "What makes the clouds move in the sky?" and, "What happens to a flower when it dies?"

Perhaps most satisfying of all this year, your two-year-old's experiences with other children have prepared her for a sea change in her relationships with peers. As she played side by side, and increasingly face to face, with children her age and older, she observed other children's behavior patterns and began to imitate them. By the end of the year, her interest in other children has probably fully asserted itself. She enjoys getting together with others her age and may even have become interested in the concept of having a "friend." As she enters her fourth year, she will particularly treasure her connections to one or two specific children and will learn a great deal from her time with them. Depending on her temperament, she may even benefit from a preschool, group-care situation, or a "threes and fours" gymnastics or music class.

LISTENING AND RESPONDING: WHAT YOU HAVE LEARNED

This third year of your life as a parent has also been full of great discoveries. Over the past twelve months, you have learned which of your own and your partner's traits your child has picked up, and you've spotted some personality quirks that are her very own. You've seen where her temperament and yours rub up against each other now and then, and where they meld perfectly. You've used your lifelong experience dealing with your personal traits—shyness, an abundance of energy, a tendency to be a night owl—to help your child adjust to her own. Meanwhile, your close observation of her physical, mental, and emotional growth has helped you adjust your parenting style to her changing needs and capabilities. As she has established herself as a presence in your home, you have moved to make room for her. Now much more than before, your relationship consists of two individuals communicating, reaching compromises, and using one another as springboards for further growth.

This trend will continue as your child enters her fourth year. Her leaps in verbal ability will greatly enhance your interaction, putting her on a more equal footing as the two of you continue to work toward her further development. The more she is able to tell you about how she feels, what she needs, and how she views the world, the better you'll be able to understand and support her, and the richer your own experience will be. Certainly, in the next year, the truism that "the child raises the parent" will become even clearer as so much of the care, energy, and thought you've put into raising your child comes back to reward you (as well as challenge you) many times over.

COMING ATTRACTIONS: DEVELOPMENTS IN THE FOURTH YEAR

One of the key concepts in the life of a three-year-old is independence. Your child's insistence on "doing it herself" this past year will result in her new ability to put on her shoes and even get a snack from the refrigerator without your help—though her shoes may end up on the wrong feet and you may not approve of the snack. Her physical coordination will improve enormously next year. She will be able to ride a tricycle, jump, and even hop on one foot, though it may still take quite a bit of concentration. Her fine-motor development will also improve—she will more frequently draw recognizable outlines of things instead of simply scribbling. All of these advances in physical and cognitive mastery please your child enormously, making her easier to get along with (much of the time) and more eager and able to please.

One of the greatest leaps your child will take next year will be in the realm of her imagination. Her ability to model real and fictional worlds in her mind will improve tremendously in the months to come. As a result, she will be able to work out a number of her emotional, social, and cognitive conflicts through pretend play, storytelling, and other mental activities. New fears will most likely surface as her imagination increases, but she will begin to settle on ways to handle these fears. She may even invent a fantasy friend next year to use as a scapegoat for bad behavior, help work out emotional dilemmas, and provide herself with a playmate who's always available on demand.

As her verbal skills continue to improve (a typical three-year-old's speaking vocabulary is between three hundred and nine hundred words), she will ask questions constantly about how the world works, where important people in her life are right now, and what she will do today. Her questions will be a sign of her continued cognitive development, which will allow her to explore her world on a much deeper level than before. Her curiosity will make her quite an interesting conversationalist and enhance her social life. Certainly by the middle of the year, she will be able to play more agreeably, to share, and to enjoy such social delights as secrets and surprises. She will be fully aware of her gender and will probably gravitate toward friends of her own sex. Her increasing ability to focus on one activity for a longer period of time will allow her to start playing more structured games, such as tag or "Go Fish." For all these reasons, more group activity, such as a preschool program or a gymnastics class, can open new vistas for her, helping her get to know herself better as well as learning more about others. By the end of the year, your more experienced three-year-old is likely to comment frequently and affectionately on herself as an individual, as in, "I *hate* potatoes," and, "I *love* dogs."

Of course, it won't all be smooth sailing in the fourth year. Parents often tell me they are surprised by the extent to which three-year-olds continue the defiant, resistant behavior they are better known for at age two. Unfortunately, their determination to have their way is a necessary part of moving toward creating their own routines, rules, and limits. Like many of us, they tend toward inflexibility while in the early stages of learning this new skill. (Think of how *you* react when your partner "helps" you as you struggle with a difficult new recipe or try to program the VCR.) Other behavior issues may come to the fore as your child enters preschool or another group situation. Other adults' negative responses to your child's actions may call your attention to issues you hadn't noticed before. Such incidents are unpleasant for any parent, of course, but they also provide a chance to help your child fine-tune her social skills and to address problems that had become so familiar you no longer noticed them.

Assisting your child on the road toward successful interaction with others, and supporting her in her continuing eagerness to learn about her world, will probably remain your prime goals for most of the coming year. Your three-year-old's better language skills, improved impulse control, relaxing focus on herself, and increasing ability to understand rational explanations will eventually help her win the struggle between babyish outbursts and more socialized behavior. As the year draws to a close, she will develop stronger resources with which to cope with such new demands as extended group activity and the need to obey rules—even when you're not around to remind her. She will be equipped with a hard-won sense of right and wrong and may well enjoy pointing out others' good and bad behavior. Best of all, she will understand that even when she does have problems with others or with herself, you and other loving adults will be there to help her see the way toward greater mastery.

FIRST-PERSON SINGULAR

Before you put this book away, remember to look back at the predictions you wrote for your child when she was twenty-four months old. Chances are your predictions were more accurate this year than the year before. As the months passed and your child's temperament and personality became increasingly clear, you were able to observe and understand her with a much more educated eye. Still, there were probably a number of ways in which your child surprised you, whether through a new behavior quirk or remarkable progress in an area of development where she had lagged before. Now that you have a better sense of who she is, get out your videotapes and photographs of your two-year-old, marvel at her progress, and think about where you want her to go. What are your goals for her, for yourself as a parent, and for your family as a whole next year? How would you most like to see your child grow? Have you noticed any particularly strong skills in your child that you might help her start to develop in the coming months? As we've seen, the better you know your unique child, the better equipped you will be to encourage her growth in the future. Thinking about her with pen in hand provides you with tools for a better future as well as precious souvenirs for the years ahead.

_____

_____

_____

_____

_____

_____

_____

_____

_____

_____

_____

_____

_____

_____

_____

_____

_____

_____

_____

_____

BIBLIOGRAPHY

Begley, Sharon. "Your Child's Brain." *Newsweek*, February 19, 1996.

Brazelton, T. Berry. *Touchpoints: Your Child's Emotional and Behavioral Development.* Reading, MA: Perseus Books, 1992.

Brownlee, Shannon. "Baby Talk." *U.S. News & World Report*, June 15, 1998.

Cole, Michael, and Sheila R. Cole. *The Development of Children*, 3rd ed. New York: W. H. Freeman and Co., 1996.

Dunn, Judy. *The Beginnings of Social Understanding.* Cambridge, MA: Harvard University Press, 1988.

Epstein, Randi Hutter. "Fix Speech Problems Early, Experts Now Urge." *New York Times*, November 30, 1999.

"Fertile Minds." *Time*, February 3, 1997.

Gopnik, Alison M., Andrew N. Meltzoff, and Patricia K. Kuhl. *The Scientist in the Crib: Minds, Brains, and How Children Learn.* New York: William Morrow & Co., 1999.

Hancock, LynNell, and Pat Wingert. "The New Preschool." *Newsweek*, February 19, 1996.

Jabs, Carolyn. "Computers and Kids." *Sesame Street Parents* (November 1999).

Lieberman, Alicia. *The Emotional Life of the Toddler.* New York: Free Press, 1993.

Markman, Ellen M. *Categorization and Naming in Children: Problems of Induction.* MIT Press Series in Learning, Development, and Conceptual Change. Cambridge, MA: Bradford Books,1991.

Newcombe, Nora. *Child Development: Change over Time.* New York: HarperCollins, 1996.

Perry, Bruce D. "Gray Matter." *Forbes*, November 30, 1998.

Pinker, Steven. *Words and Rules: The Ingredients of Language.* New York: Basic Books, 1999.

"Read*Write*Now*." Available at: www.ed.gov.

Rhodes, Sonya, with Lee Lusardi Connor. "Discipline ABCs." *Sesame Street Parents* (November, 1999).

Shore, Rima. *Rethinking the Brain: New Insights into Early Development*. New York: Families and Work Institute, 1997.

Sroufe, L. Alan, Robert G. Cooper, and Ganie B. Dehart. *Child Development: Its Nature and Course*, 4th ed. New York: McGraw-Hill, 2000.

Stern, Daniel N. *Diary of a Baby: What Your Child Sees, Feels, and Experiences*. New York: Basic Books, 1998.

Windell, James. *Discipline: A Sourcebook of Fifty Failsafe Techniques for Parents*. New York: Macmillan, 1991.

"Your Child: From Birth to Three." *Newsweek Special Issue* (Fall-Winter 2000).

RECOMMENDED READING

CHAPTER ONE: **WHAT I'M LIKE**
Brazelton, T. Berry. *Touchpoints: Your Child's Emotional and Behavioral Development.* Reading, MA: Perseus Books, 1992.

American Academy of Pediatrics, Steven Shelov (ed.), Robert E. Hanneman (ed.), and Catherine D. De Angelis (ed.). *Caring for Your Baby and Young Child: Birth to Age Five.* New York: Bantam Doubleday Dell, 1998.

CHAPTER TWO: **JUMP, COLOR, AND DANCE—MY PHYSICAL ABILITIES**
Spock, Benjamin, and Stephen J. Parker, *Dr. Spock's Baby and Child Care,* 7th ed. New York: Pocket Books, 1998.

CHAPTER THREE: **CREATING A WORLD—MY COGNITIVE DEVELOPMENT**
Gardner, Howard. *Frames of Mind: The Theory of Multiple Intelligences,* 10th anniversary ed. New York: Basic Books, 1993.

Greenspan, Stanley, and Serena Weider, with Robin Simon. *The Child with Special Needs: Encouraging Intellectual and Emotional Growth.* Reading, MA: Perseus Books, 1998.

CHAPTER FOUR: **"I SEED A PLANE!"—MY VERBAL ABILITIES**
Gopnik, Alison M., Andrew N. Meltzoff, and Patricia K. Kuhl. *The Scientist in the Crib: Minds, Brains, and How Children Learn.* New York: William Morrow & Co., 1999.

Pinker, Steven. *The Language Instinct: How the Mind Creates Language.* New York: HarperPerennial, 1995.

Pinker, Steven. *Words and Rules: The Ingredients of Language.* New York: Basic Books, 1999.

CHAPTER FIVE: **PRIDE AND ANXIETY—MY EMOTIONAL GROWTH**

Chess, Stella, and Alexander Thomas. *Know Your Child*. New York: Basic Books, 1987.

Greenspan, Stanley, and Nancy Thorndike Greenspan. *First Feelings: Milestones in the Emotional Development of your Baby and Child*. New York: Viking, 1985.

Kagan, Jerome. *The Nature of the Child*. New York: Basic Books, 1984.

Lieberman, Alicia. *The Emotional Life of the Toddler*. New York: Free Press, 1993.

Pruett, Kyle. *Fatherneed: Why Father Care Is as Essential as Mother Care for Your Child*. New York: Free Press, 2000.

CHAPTER SIX: **"PLAY WITH ME!"—MY SOCIAL DEVELOPMENT**

Dunn, Judy. *The Beginnings of Social Understanding*. Cambridge, MA: Harvard University Press, 1988.

Greenspan, Stanley, with Jacqueline Salmon. *The Challenging Child: Understanding, Raising, and Enjoying the Five "Difficult" Types of Children*. Reading, MA: Addison-Wesley, 1997.

Kagan, Jerome, and Sharon Lamb, eds. *The Emergence of Morality in Young Children*. Chicago: University of Chicago Press, 1988.

CHAPTER SEVEN: **A STABLE PLATFORM—MY NEED FOR ROUTINE**

Robert, Susan B.:, Melvin Heyman, and Lisa Tracy. *Feeding Your Child for Lifelong Health: Birth Through Age Six*. New York: Bantam, 1999.

Wilkoff, William G. *Coping with a Picky Eater: A Guide for the Perplexed Parent*. New York: Simon and Schuster, 1998).

CHAPTER EIGHT: **"BUT I WANT TO!"—MY NEED FOR LIMITS**

Brazelton, T. Berry, *Touchpoints: Your Child's Emotional and Behavioral Development*. Reading, MA: Perseus Books, 1992.

Windell, James. *Discipline: A Sourcebook of Fifty Failsafe Techniques for Parents*. New York: Macmillan, 1991.

ORGANIZATIONS AND
SUPPORT GROUPS

ADVICE AND RESOURCES FOR PARENTS
Family Resource Coalition
(312) 338–0900
Chicago, IL
This service puts callers in touch with state and local branches for accessible community support.

National Parent Information Network
(800) 583–4135
Largest parenting database in the United States. Parents can call for free professional referrals, advice, and printed articles. Weekdays, 8:00 A.M. to 5:00 P.M. (CST).

Zero to Three
734 15th Street NW, Suite 1000
Washington, DC 20005
(202) 638–1144
www.zerotothree.org
Call this child advocacy group for a general information kit, or access the website for excellent information on all aspects of infant and toddler development.

Online Resources
American Academy of Pediatrics
www.aap.org
The academy provides a wealth of information on the most recent scientific findings on teething, nightmares, toilet training, and countless other issues affecting children and their families.

Babycenter.com

www.babycenter.com

This website provides frequent updates on your child's development, as well as answers to parents' questions and a large database of information for parents.

Connect for Kids

www.connectforkids.org

An action and information center for citizens, businesses, and parents who want to make their communities work for kids.

Family.com

www.family.com

Sponsored by Disney, this website provides forums for parents to meet and talk online.

ParenTalk Newsletter

www.tnpc.com/parentalk/index.html

An online collection of articles by psychologists and physicians for parents.

ParenthoodWeb

www.parenthoodweb.com

Answers to frequently asked questions. Pediatricians and psychiatrists also respond to parents' questions sent by e-mail.

Parenting Q&A

www.parenting-qa.com

Offers answers to parents' questions, reading lists and activity suggestions for kids, and other family services.

ParentSoup

www.parentsoup.com

A good source of online advice for parents for nearly every challenging situation.

U.S. Department of Education

www.ed.gov

Provides ideas and resources for parents relating to early childhood education, including the excellent Read*Write*Now* Early Childhood Kit.

Child Care Aware
National Association for Child Care Resource and Referral Agencies
1319 F Street NW, Suite 810
Washington, DC 20004
(800) 424–2246
www.naccrra.net
Child Care Aware provides referrals to local licensed and accredited child-care centers anywhere in the United States. It also offers a free information packet on how to choose quality child care. Weekdays, 9:00 A.M. to 4:30 P.M. (EST).

Families and Work Institute
330 Seventh Avenue
New York, NY 10001
(212) 465–2044
www.familiesandwork.org
Publishers of the excellent book for parents and professionals, *Rethinking the Brain: New Insights into Early Development* by Rima Shore, this organization provides information relating to the changing nature of work and family life.

SPECIAL NEEDS

Mothers United for Mutual Support
150 Custer Court
Green Bay, WI 54301
(414) 336–5333
Support and networking for families of children with any disorder, delay, or disability.

National Organization of Mothers of Twins Club
PO Box 23188
Albuquerque, NM 87192–1188
(505) 275–0955
Offers advice and information to parents of twins and refers callers to local chapters.

CRISIS INTERVENTION
ChildHelp National Hotline

(800) 4–A–CHILD

Twenty-four-hour advice and referrals from counselors with graduate degrees for children and adults with questions or in crisis.

National Clearinghouse for Family Support/Children's Mental Health
(800) 628–1696

Twenty-four-hour information and referrals to local family clinics, support groups, and therapists.

SUPPORT GROUPS

National Association of Mothers' Centers
336 Fulton Avenue
Hempstead, NY 11550
(800) 645–3828

Provides referrals to mothers' support groups and centers in your area, as well as information on how to start a group.

Parents Anonymous
Claremont, CA
(909) 621–6184
(800) 932–HOPE

Provides referrals to state and local affiliates, which offer support groups, counseling, and referrals. Weekdays, 8:00 A.M. to 4:30 P.M. (PST).

Parents Without Partners
401 North Michigan Avenue
Chicago, IL 60611
(312) 644–6610

National organization with local chapters providing support for single parents.

INDEX

Page numbers in *italics* refer to illustrations.

naps, 137, 177, 180, 181–82
National Institute of Mental Health, 70
nature vs. nurture, 101, 105, 128
needs and motivations, of child, 24
neural nets, 101
Newsweek, 79
"no":
   child's saying of, 12, 89, 121
   parent's saying of, 223, 226

object permanence, 64
objects, classifying of, 16
one-year-olds, two-year-olds compared with,
   9, 11, 18, 95
organizations and support groups, 247–50

parenting advice, 2, 4
parents:
   child's activity level and, 39, 41–42
   child's gender-related attitudes derived
     from, 159–60
   in child's social development, 147,
     152–55, 168–69
   child's testing of responses of, 153,
     181
   child's verbal growth aided by, 23, 97–99,
     99
   controlling own anger by, 227–28
   decreased importance of "teaching" role
     of, 4
   disagreements between, 213–16
   general pointers for, 22–24
   hourly rate of conflicts between children
     and, 117
   importance of consistency on part of,
     129–30, 209–10, 213, 226
   paying attention to child's signals as job
     of, 22, 45
   praise given to child by, 124–25
   on setting limits, 208–9
   supporting child's interests as role of, 7,
     14
   temperamental differences between child
     and, 128–29
   what you have learned, 238–39

Parent's Story sections:
   on cognitive development, 59–60
   on emotional growth, 122
   on physical skills, 34–35
   on social development, 148–49
   on thinking like a toddler, 14–15
   on transition to sleeping alone, 182–83
   on verbal skills, 92–93
personality, emergence and building of,
     24–25, 117, 126–30, *127*, 235
physical abilities, 2, 9, 11, 29–54
   Child's-Eye View of, 45–46
   developmental delays in, 37–38
   early motor achievements, 32–34
   fine-motor, 11, 30–31, 33, 52–53, 239
   First-Person Singular and Reader's Notes
     sections on, 53–54
   in fourth year, 239
   getting to know the body, 46–47
   gross-motor, 11, 30, 36, 52–53
   learning to maneuver in a big kids' world,
     50–51
   learning to move with others, 48–49
   link between cognitive skills and, 34
   refining of, 38–41
   in third year, 52–53
   time off for, 42
physical punishment, 215, 220, 225–27
physiological development, 11
Piaget, Jean, 58
Pinker, Steven, 100
planning ahead, to avoid trouble, 21, 36, 39,
     40, 121, 137, 220–22, 227–28
play, social development through, 156–61,
     158
play areas, household, 39–40
play dates, 9, 42, 81, 145–46, 150, 161–62,
     171–72
playgrounds, 51, 165–66
"Post Office," 71
practice, *see* repetition and practice
praise, 124–25, 190–91
premature children, 102
preoperational phase, 59
preschool, 79–81, 159, 160